Root & Branch

EDA GUNAYDIN is a Turkish-Australian essayist and re-searcher, whose writing explores class, capital, intergenerational trauma and diaspora. You can find her work in the *Sydney Review of Books*, *Meanjin*, *The Lifted Brow* and others. She has been a finalist for a Queensland Literary Award and the Scribe Nonfiction Prize. *Root & Branch* is her debut essay collection.

'In *Root & Branch*, Eda Gunaydin's essays showcase the fine craft of a writer whose seemingly dispassionate observations set a wide stage for astute, deeply considered reflections on place, people, politics and power. It takes immense skill to weave personal narratives seamlessly into broader conversations and complex social commentary. To do so in an effortless manner, as Gunaydin has accomplished, is pure alchemy. This is a book I will revisit many times for both the beauty of its language and for the generous opportunities to think and learn alongside the writer. A moving, thought-provoking and truly stunning debut.'

EILEEN CHONG

'*Root & Branch* is a book of autobiographical essays that pay careful attention to, in Gunaydin's words, "the materiality of living": sore feet, varicose veins, fast food and other everyday events in working-class life. It is also funny, self-deprecating, self-dramatising and hopeful: a searching and multi-faceted debut.'

ANWEN CRAWFORD

'Julia Kristeva once wrote that "You are a genius to the extent that you are able to challenge the sociohistorical conditions of your identity." Identity not in its censual use, i.e. sex, class, religion; identity rather as the set of ideologies we carry with us: the spirit of an age, the normative practices of personhood, language and narrative, and the bromides of accepted wisdom. The Eda of Gunaydin's formidable essays is shrewd, compassionate, revolutionary, and yes, unmistakably a genius. This book is the exorcism I've been waiting for.'

ELLENA SAVAGE

'Gunaydin's work, and it is work, lands with a deceptive lightness on the page and its readers. Its weight grows on us over time – reminders of the daily inheritance of trauma, responsibility and structures over which we can only sometimes wrest control. Forget vital or necessary. *Root & Branch* is knowing and real. In every essay, Eda circles something much bigger than the sum of her experience and thought, as both witness and participant, in which we as readers are left guessing our place.'

ALISON WHITTAKER

'What has always struck me about Eda Gunaydin's essays is their remarkable and balanced movement, the deft way they bring together a fierce intelligence and political consciousness with a depth and complexity of feeling, as well as a wicked sense of humour and of the absurd. They are forthright and passionate, but also playful, cynical and sharp, and keenly interested in all of the ordinary ways that extraordinary historical and social forces are felt across our lives, and what it means to both bear and resist their weight.'

FIONA WRIGHT

'Gunaydin is a gifted essayist driven by an honest desire to see society transformed, "to alter the conditions of everyday existence, so that there's nothing that we need to be saved from". Gunaydin's ability to combine a searing intellect with wit and ingenuity is breathtaking.'

BOOKS + PUBLISHING

Root & Branch

Essays on inheritance

Eda Gunaydin

NEWSOUTH

A NewSouth book

Published by
NewSouth Publishing
University of New South Wales Press Ltd
University of New South Wales
Sydney NSW 2052
AUSTRALIA
https://unsw.press

A catalogue record for this book is available from the National Library of Australia

ISBN   9781742237312 (paperback)
            9781742238395 (ebook)
            9781742239293 (ePDF)

Internal design Josephine Pajor-Markus
Cover design Alissa Dinallo

Contents

A Rock Is A Hard Place

Mum wants to eat Turkish food. She always wants to eat Turkish food.

'Lütfen,' she implores, every weekend. 'Benim hatırım için. Yoksa çok yalnız kalıyorum.' I fancy that I can save her from loneliness by choking down iskender together once a week. It's sacrificial lamb.

Her kebab place of choice is on Blacktown's Main Street. I know there are eight kebab places on Main Street. I mean the Turkish place. Not the kebab place run by the Afghans or Lebanese. You can pick it out because it sells Turkish bread, not Afghan or Lebanese bread. And you can tell it from the amcas and yenges without jobs and with heart conditions who sit out front sculling black tea all day, holding sugar cubes in their cheeks while they gulp and gossip and argue. They slide into the back to prepare fresh cups, and don't pay for them come bill time.

Before the doorbell can tinkle, Barış is in motion. Barış is the owner of a kebab shop on Main Street. He runs his own HSP Appreciation page, on which he posts photographs of the HSPs he makes: packed, stuffed, laden things, layers of chips and meat crammed into a pizza box – something I know, from experience, weighs at least two kilos and which it feels improbable that someone is supposed to eat, although it is possible this is a form of cultural cringe. He captions his creations with text written on the box lid in barbecue sauce.

Barış is also the one who said I dress like a slut, last week, I think in retaliation for my yelling at him for making fun of the girl who was burned to death in a minibus. The minibus in Turkey, I mean. So many minibus murders it's hard to keep track. So is he really polite if he doesn't charge for tea? I don't know. I don't make the rules.

'Teyze!' he says. Drops the veritable machete he uses to strip meat from the rotisserie, scrambles out from behind the counter, snaps up the used plates from our table and disappears them into the back. I can see he is on his best behaviour, not because anyone has attempted to avenge me for the slut comment, but rather because during the course of that same conversation with my mother, while I was still out of earshot, he also happened to call my sister Dilek fat. I imagine him saying something like, 'Oh, the fat one or the slut one?' and have to contain my laughter about how much of an arsehole you have to be. When my mother told my father what had occurred, it angered him so much that he drove to Barış's shop in the evening, fresh off work, wearing his steel-capped boots, and kicked the man in the leg. I don't see why I should have to contain my mirth over that story, which I view as functionally perfect in every way: the image of the kicking, my sister's pleading face, both hurt and begging my father not to react.

Still, teyze is the right thing for him to say. My mother likes it when they call her teyze and ignore their white and black customers to make us shitty coffee on the espresso machine Barış bought from a school canteen, to class up the place. She likes it when she can order for me rather than me for her. We take a seat on red pleather chairs with cigarette burns in them. We never sit outside because she says there are Kurds in front. I don't know. I don't make the rules.

It doesn't bother me as much today. It's January and this way we don't have to be under the sun. In Turkish we say güneşin alnı. On the forehead of the sun. It's a malapropism – the phrase for 'under the sun' is güneşin altı. But I prefer the former because it's funny. I like to be able to like and to know something about Turkish, besides the fucking food.

Mum reaches out to smack me on the knee.

'Lezbiyenler gibi oturuyorsun yine. Kahvedeki adamlar gibi.'

I'm sitting like a lesbian again. Mothers always know. Or I'm sitting like some grizzled man at a coffeehouse spinning a tespih through my fingers, playing endless games of tavla with my grizzled man friends. My mother has never sat in any way other than with one ankle tucked behind the other, pleats straight, and a gold brooch doing that thing of drawing-not-drawing attention to her tits.

'Aren't *you* a lesbian now?' I say. I'm ribbing. I've just found out she went to Erkek Ayşe's house last week. They tried on dresses together. Erkek Ayşe has permanently cropped hair which she has cut at the barber on Main Street. She is always in a vest. Her upper left arm permanently bulging from how she stores her cigarettes, in the sleeve of her t-shirt. We call her Erkek Ayşe. Like the way there's too many Kemals so we call one Bald Kemal, the other Funny Kemal. Fat Ahmet, Plasterer Ahmet. Erkek Ayşe is Man Ayşe. I don't make the rules.

'The woman is married,' my mother insists. Holds out her fingers and looks at her wedding ring with a little moue of her own.

'You hung out in your underwear together,' I remind her, sip my cappuccino and try to un-lesbian my legs as a gesture of good will.

Erkek Ayşe is sitting outside, in fact. Mum had breezed past with no greeting.

'I bet she's mad at me.' My mother snickers.

'For what?' I say. 'Did you not let her down gently?'

I look out the window to soak in her butch realness one more time. At this, Ayşe notices us and stands, pointing a crooked finger at Mum the whole time she's marching up. She scrapes back the third chair at our table and drops in.

'Bersa,' she announces.

'Besra,' says Mum. Ayşe gets it wrong every time, I think – hope – on purpose. Any woman who can knock my mother down a notch, for me, hangs the moon.

'You know I don't like to speak your language,' she says, in Mum's language. She sniffs. 'Your government tried to make it illegal but I still spoke only Kurdish till I was eight years old.' She leans into her accent.

4

'It's not illegal,' says Mum immediately. 'Who told you it was?'

'My uncle, who was taken political prisoner for teaching Kurmanji,' says Erkek Ayşe. 'Listen. We have to talk about what you posted on Face.' What Turks call Facebook. My mother is a notorious sharer of nationalist memes – horny poetry about Atatürk, flags flapping, genocide denial. 'I keep saying that we'd be great friends if you just posted your selfies and Mahjong games and that's it.'

Mum interrupts.

'Look, Ayşe, I know we are friends –' I want to say they call each other *friend* too often for there not to be homoeroetic subtext but it's not the right time. I'm an expert at taking the piss, but less sure about where to put the piss I collect. '– but you have to understand. Ben Atatürkçüyüm, ben cumhuriyetçiyim ve bunu benden alamazsın.'

'No one is trying to take away your Kemalism,' says Erkek Ayşe. She is idyllically calm. I can see the others watching us.

Mum interrupts again.

'I have to insist on this, Ayşe. If you do not love the republic that doesn't mean I shouldn't. What happened when the Greeks were putting our Turkish babies on pikes? Atatürk threw them back into the sea! Shouldn't I be proud?'

'Tamam, Berva,' says Erkek Ayşe. 'All right. Afiyet olsun.'

Her retreat is dignified but the air is crackling. I think we might get punched.

'Kürt inadı gibi hiçbir şey görmedim. Kurdish stubbornness is something else. I knew she'd react like that. My big mouth. I'm so naughty, aren't I?'

Mum stands to retrieve a copy of *Hürriyet* newspaper from the stand by the door, which she unfurls imperiously. Imperialistically. She searches through her purse, at leisure and without sparing a look up or outside, retrieves her reading glasses, slides them up her nose, and cracks into solving the crossword.

The amcas and yenges are still watching us. One of them makes to stand but Erkek Ayşe tugs him back down. I pull my gaze to Mum, clear my throat, and can't help but laugh.

*

'Abla,' Barış says, approaching with two mugs of tea. He wipes his hands on his apron. 'Abla, could I ask you for a favour?'

Funny that he's calling me Abla even though I am a lot younger than him. I take it as a sign he is eager to sweep my alleged sluttiness under the rug. Or, it occurs to me, what is just as likely is that he never called me a slut at all, and that my mother has made up the story, thinking it will help to alter my mode of dress in some way, as if it is incumbent upon me to care about what every second dry-dick rando in the Turkish community thinks or feels. It's a joke, of course, because my mother, like all women, understands, I know she understands, what it feels like to have your *name out there,* that is, to be spoken about in a sexist way on the streets. I suspect this is why she enforces the rules so zealously: doesn't sit with the men the way that Erkek Ayşe does, and never goes to the coffee shop three doors down, which has been converted into an ersatz kahve, where men and some of the women go to play tavla.

'Would you do me a favour? My sister has been here since May. She has a university degree like you. She's an electrical engineering graduate. But she can't find a job. She speaks perfect English, I promise. She has taken classes. She has a degree! And she can work with her visa. Her English is not like mine, abla. She has a degree. You probably know of lots of jobs.'

'Oh,' I say. I am instantly desperate to fix his sister's life, planning out my own heroism. 'Um, sure. Facebook'tan eklesin beni.'

'Allah razı olsun,' he says. 'God bless you.'

I am not equipped to help Suzan, although I try. I ask Justin to look over her CV, and he provides feedback the same way he did for me when I was nineteen and we had first started dating. I send her a few links to jobs. She tells me she wants to go home but Barış has three kids and a shop to run and he needs her here. I play with fonts and indents. I email her back the document, but don't hear from her.

*

'Don't be a haram dingo.'

Suzan makes a note on the order pad to look up the phrase when she gets home. The two guys jostle each other and rant at full volume about the best combination of sauces to choose. She stares into the middle distance until they pick their three, says all the numbers in their change correctly, and the one says to the other, 'Mate, we're going to be late to class,' and they leave.

She squeezes the last of the lemons, the juice by now

having seeped into the tiny cuts on her fingers, small sores that she worries open with her teeth when she's hidden in the back of the shop. She pops an olive into her mouth. Suzan sucks on them when she's bored. They're what pass as stimulation during quiet periods. She scrolls on her phone with a gloved finger, alternating between SkyScanner – looking up flight prices – and cycling through Instagram, through her boyfriend's photos, through photos of her friends from uni. It's snowing in Trabzon.

*

I chuck a small shit fit the day I don't get a position I'd interviewed for to do 'media at an office', as I describe it to my mother. She aims to console and so says something placating like, 'Well, why wouldn't they hire you, what could the other girl have had over you?'

I know the girl that got hired, the white girl. I chalk it up to the fact that her mother had scored her two summer internships at high profile publications in the past. The hiring organisation had been wowed by her communications background.

I say it to soothe myself and not my mother, who has never had a job in this country except cleaning, so how could such a miniature injustice smart?

Mum still says sorry. 'In Turkey I could have gotten you a job.' Her voice cracks. 'Orada adamdım ama burada – I'm nothing, sorry. Nothing olmayı sevmiyorum.'

*

8

Hortlak, thinks Besra. She hates her sister-in-law. Out loud she just says, 'Thanks. Janine, thanks.'

Twice because people struggle to understand her *th-*. At the butcher when Besra asks for three kilos she gets two about half the time. It throws off the dinners she cooks for the household and makes Mehmet and Janine and their kids complain, so she serves her husband and daughter a little less on those days.

'Oh, don't even mention it,' says Janine. She is on the red couch covered in plastic, legs crossed so tightly she can wrap one ankle around the other. 'It was really dad that got you the job. He vouched for you because I asked him to.'

'Thanks, Janine. Thanks.'

'You have to work in this country,' she comments. 'You can't just squeeze out babies.'

Janine picks a piece of lint off her leggings, uncrosses her legs and wanders over to the fridge. She pokes through the freezer and then turns back around.

'You forgot to fill this again.' She bangs the last two cubes out of the ice cube tray. 'Now my ice water is going to be warm.'

'I am sorry,' Besra says. Amına koyduğumun hortlağı.

*

Janine's father is assigned as Besra's supervisor. He sources her a uniform a size too large, or she's lost weight since coming here. She hems and cinches the dress with a shade of blue string that doesn't quite match the baby blue hue the cleaners wear. But it's what's available at the Salvation Army.

'What a waist you have on you,' says Joel. 'Even with a kid. Tell you what, Janine's mum did not look like this. She's where Janine got her horse face from.'

She agrees about the woman's horse face but thinks Joel is a buruşuk piç. She cleans toilet after toilet and resolves to pass the clerical qualifying with top marks.

*

The man that Joel calls Big Boss arrives for a meeting with Centre Management. Joel calls her over and they stand side-by-side appraising her.

'This is Bess,' says Joel. 'She's my son-in-law's sister. My daughter's got the whole clan living with them while they settle in.'

'Welcome,' says Big Boss. 'Where you from then?'

Besra clears her throat.

'Turk-Turkey.'

'Turk Turkey, huh?' says Big Boss. He and Joel laugh. 'Only kidding, love. You know what? I've actually been there once. Civilised bunch. You guys know hospitality.'

'Thanks, thanks.'

Big Boss hears *tanks* and so turns away to say something about Tiananmen Square from the news to Joel. She practises the *th-*, *th-* as she buses trays left behind in the food court. The sight of French fries makes her queasy.

*

Joel brings her into the utility room in her second week. She's always conscious he'll corner her – that any man will corner her. Korkma. Korkma.

All he says is, 'Bess. Can you get the spill by the Price Attack on level 2?'

She prepares the trolley while he watches. Even comes up the elevator with her. Besra wonders if he thinks she's behind the thefts of purses from the food court. Adi herif.

The puddle is off-yellow.

'Think it's tea or something?' asks Joel.

Besra shrugs and pulls out the mop. It's a busy day for the Westfield, Saturday and noon. Mums in large bright blocky blazers motor past, some clutching the hand of a kid with straw-coloured hair or a Push Pop held in their mouth. Men in boots with tattoos on their shins spill en masse out of the Bottle Mart, cases of beer propped over a shoulder. Perhaps Joel is here because he knows how she avoids the messes in thoroughfares, where these people endlessly ask her for directions to stores, as if she is also the concierge or kapıcı. She puts her head down and lets her hair fall into her face to ward off their evil eyes. She thinks about what hairdo she'll use for her secretarial interview next week. Once her shift ends she will try a couple different styles, and use Janine's vanity out of spite.

Joel loses patience in the end.

'What, doesn't your nose work? It's piss, woman! It's piss.'

He says it loud enough for the passers-by to hear. She doesn't notice if they do or do not laugh, but knowing Australia she remembers it in the affirmative. Their evil eyes.

Joel says: 'Your face. The look on your face.'

Tham comes up to help after Joel's radio calls him away, the mirth of the situation having fizzled. Besra had seen the woman's name new on the roster below hers, and contemplates greeting her, welcoming her to the job. But she doesn't have the th- down. Doesn't want to mispronounce the poor woman's name. Doesn't have the energy either way. Ayrıca, she thinks, ikimiz de burada olmak istemiyoruz. She doesn't play out the charade, of this being a real job.

*

The last time I visit the kebab shop on Main Street with my mother, I am still working at a wine store in the Inner West. The work is pretentious – I get into the habit of buying and drinking entire bottles for the purposes of 'homework', swirling, aspirating, spitting, convincing myself I am tasting what I think I am tasting. Cherries, bananas, whatever: the customers believe me, generally, no matter what I say. It's a confidence game. My mother has wheeled me in this day specifically because she has had another disagreement with Barış, this one, in my view, much more insubstantial than the last.

'Go,' says my mother. 'Tell him.' She wants me to explain to him what penalty rates are: the last time she came by to do her crossword she had remarked that I made thirty-one dollars an hour on Sundays, and he had refused to believe it, accused me of being a liar. I think it's quaint that this man is so obsessed with me, but really I wonder if it's because he makes or pays his staff much less than what I receive.

I refuse, because I have to find ways to entertain myself when locked in this spiral with my mother. The spiral is her obsessiveness as it comes up against what she calls my stubbornness, which I didn't inherit from her, but from my father. I am interested in how selectively some traits are attributed to her children. Kürt inadı, Alevi inadı. When I say I have the latter, to give myself a giggle, she just looks at me, deathly serious, and says, 'No, I don't think of you as Alevi. Sen benim kızımsın.'

I have no choice but to find my mother's way of responding to my refusal amusing – her knack for saving nothing in reserve, blowing her load instantly and going nuclear over even small things, like this.

'Allah aşkına,' she says. 'Lütfen. Beni seviyorsan.'

I don't know if I do.

'Why even tell him where I work?' I ask. Still resentful. 'Isn't drinking for whores?'

'You know I think you're better than that job,' she says.

'Well, I'm not,' I say. 'It's the job that I could find so it's the job that I have.'

Barış steps out from the back, spots us, throws a tea towel over his shoulder and comes by our table.

'Nasılsın yenge?'

My mother shrugs, looks at me expectantly. I stare back like a stubborn fool.

'Bize taze taze bir peynirli ıspanaklı gözleme hazırlar

mısın?' she says, speaks to him as if he were a stranger, and not a friend whose establishment she has patronised at least once a week for a couple of years. God, I wish she could keep friends. For my sake, not theirs.

He says, 'Tabii,' and wanders off. I know at the end of this meal when he calculates our bill he will knock off a few dollars out of respect, and my mother will still say, *No, no, no,* and pay the full amount.

'I never said you were a whore,' says my mother. 'Just that people will think you are.' A distinction without a difference.

'O zaman bize başörtüsü taktırsaydın.' I say.

My mother scrunches her nose.

'Biz Araplar gibi değiliz.'

'Oh, really?' I say. Feeling shitty. I throw my hands up behind my head in an act of bravado. Decide to start a fight just for the sake of it: 'I am.'

'Manyak manyak konuşma.' I've done it: made her angry. 'Her şeyi bildiğini sanıyorsun, ama namus konusunda hiç bir bok bilmiyorsun.'

*

I am preoccupied with what happens at kebab shops. In fact, the first piece of work I ever published was a short story called 'Meat'. I wrote it in 2016 when I was twenty-two, during breaks taken in between writing essays on comparative politics and political theory as I completed my undergraduate honours year in Government and International Relations. This is a field I never intended to enter, but in which, five years on, I remain. 'Meat' was my first piece of work to be accepted into a literary magazine, *Voiceworks,* a publication that has helped make my and many other young writers' careers in this country. The same year, the story was shortlisted for the Monash University Undergraduate Creative Writing Prize, although it did not win. Nevertheless, I travelled to Melbourne to attend the Emerging Writers' Festival and watch the prize be awarded (to someone else, who deserved it). I note these facts only in order to say that 'Meat' made me. Made it, anyway, so that I was someone who did several things, one of which was also writing – after 'Meat', I went to writing events and made writer connections. 'Meat' made my friends start joking, 'Will your next story be called 'chicken'? What about, 'sandwich'?' *No, no, you don't get it. It's about labour,* I kept sighing, only semi-seriously. In reality I like the ribbing.

'Meat' is cut out of life. It is peppered with little details, anecdotes, which I have tucked away over the years because of the joy that they spark in me. My favourite, which I find that my mind revisits on May Day every year, is the one about a man that my sister Gülin told me about, who worked in the Kemeraltı Çarşısı of İzmir for a former friend of hers who owned a shoe store. The shoe store owner had gotten into his head the idea that he should have his employee wear a sandwich board as a sign, functioning as a walking advertisement for the store. The practice had caused a small, city-wide scandal, so significant was the outrage of onlookers, who found the idea of making a human wear an A-frame degrading. He never did it again. I could write for a thousand years and never make up a story that better encapsulates the rage and the absurdity of life under capitalism, and our potential to push back against it.

This is only a subplot, however. 'Meat' was, in substance, about a fictional protagonist named Berna, who lived in Fremantle with her daughter Yağmur, and worked at a kebab shop. I wrote her so that Berna hated Australia, detested it in that visceral way I have observed in many migrants who came here as adults. As in the late Ania Walwicz's most well-known poem, 'Australia', Berna resents having to navigate a new tongue, and she feels alienated by the Western Australian landscape. In one scene, I have her think, with distaste, in Turkey the ruins have ruins; they have to dig up the new ruins to get to the old ruins. This is a genuinely common sentiment that I hear expressed – one of my dearest loved ones found it impossible to live here, to be here, because she could not seem to connect to the place as a place, its characteristic flatness. I feel it myself, sometimes, despite having been born here and having been lucky enough to be nourished on Dharug land, a kind of bleakness that I associate with living in a settler-colony as a settler. None of this is mine, but I have to find a way to be here. I'm supposed to find a way to live here, to be present here, and not to carry forward an inherited hatred of this country which should not belong to me: the hatred, I mean, although the country also does not belong to me. Under different circumstances I know that this would be a fecund country, not bleak or alienating at all. This is one of the central puzzles that animates me: how to be here, with no place else, realistically, to go. How not to cave to deficit thinking that tells me I am two half-people, not one whole, full person, caught between something and something else, here without really being here.

One of the ways I write is through taking extensive notes in Google Keep, which don't generally make sense, but make a kind of sense that is restrained only to those moments, as with dreams. In one, I write:

> To live as if everything were temporary is how I interact with Australia. It's also how trauma makes you interact with experiences. You're like: 'Sorry, I have to go back to my main memory now. There's something more important I have to be remembering.'

After 'Meat', another string of random events saw me sit down for the first time in front of a publisher in 2018. Although they did not go on to publish my book – which Justin and I semi-jokingly dubbed 'A Rock Is A Hard Place', although I still secretly enjoy that title – I recall sitting outdoors in front of a cafe in Parramatta, overlooking Centenary Square, me vibrating with nervous tension while they calmly walked me through their feedback on the few pieces of writing I had sent over. My fiction, in particular, they noted, was promising. They liked my unsubdued, melodramatic style. I took that to be a kind of idiosyncratic praise, my way of writing to a different, non-western literary tradition that refuses to prize repression as an aesthetic ideal, or at least plays equally with both withholding and excess. Media genres like the dizi or the telenovela or the soap opera are often deemed over the top, but, more unrealistic narrative flourishes aside, I truly believe that there are people who act and feel with something approaching the kind of intensity these modes depict. People sometimes tell me, maybe in the heat of a disagreement, *Eda, you're too much,* and I say, *well, I am Turkish,* as if that explains it.

What I mean by this is that Berna is melodramatic in the way that I think real people are. After work, she rests her feet up against a wall in bed at night because she can't sleep from the way that they ache and have swelled. She yells and swears at her daughter. She lights cigarettes off the stove. Berna is a composite character – an admixture of my father, family friends, folks I know who do work at kebab shops and who I grew up around. In the Turkish community, kebab shop owners and workers are everywhere. You can find work at a kebab shop, easily – just go to a new town or a new suburb and set one up, and you have access to a fairly ready income stream. The Australian appetite for the HSP is bottomless, although, curiously, the Australian appetite for Islam and its practitioners, who keep halal, is low.

Berna is industrious and gritty and she keeps her head down and she hustles and by the end of the story she becomes a business owner rather than just an employee. She goes on to hire her own staff. She wins the game of succeeding on this continent, within the confines of the rules as they exist. It's not a migrant success story. It's not about a woman with few opportunities in her homeland who unlocks class mobility for herself and her family by pulling up her bootstraps; I didn't want it to read as one, anyway, although I grew worried, subsequent to the story's modest success, that that is exactly what I had depicted.

I learn about the SBS documentary *Kebab Kings,* which aired in 2015 and advertised that it would lift the lid on the multicultural institution that is the kebab shop. I distrust the word multiculturalism: it seems to me to be a neat way of resolving difference by subsuming it under the mythical unity of the umbrella of the nation-state. Australia as a kind of lid, tamping down on understanding race and racism as global phenomena. This alternate understanding would require a response premised on internationalist solidarity. The Halal Snack Pack Appreciation society, a Facebook group that reached the zenith of its popularity throughout my university years, in particular in 2016, makes me cringe and roll my eyes. It's not a big deal, really – just regular Aussies reviewing snack packs, discussing ideal sauce combinations, rating the completeness of the HSP experience. Members of the group refer to one another as brother and sister. Former Labor Party Senator Sam Dastyari hams up his appreciation of the HSP. In 2016, he reaches across the aisle and offers to split one with One Nation leader Pauline Hanson. Twee puff pieces run about Dastyari's favourite HSPs. Hanson declines the offer and mounts a campaign against halal certification. Who does this theatre help? I want to know. I think that the HSP discourse is what prompted me to write 'Meat'.

For a long time, my Facebook and Twitter banner images have featured a snatch of graffiti thrown up on a wall during the 2018 Yellow Vests protests in Paris. It reads 'a bas le caviar, vive le kebab'. *Down with caviar, up with kebabs.*

I believe in their symbolic potential. But I don't really imagine the kebab, specifically the site of the kebab shop, as a utopic melting pot. I'm not anti-utopian, and I'm not a humourless person, I don't think. In fact, sometimes laughing is the only thing I can do. I criticise exactly because I want a revolution.

I watch *Kebab Kings* semi-seriously, although it's worth noting that I have no beef with the show. You see? I cracked a joke, and therefore I am not humourless. I would hazard, however, that I don't think it's worth celebrating the fact that the only times we members of the middle-class encounter working class, Black or brown people is when they are serving us food or driving us somewhere. It is bleak to contemplate how few spaces in Australian social life actually make possible the mixing of different socioeconomic classes and different races anymore. What watching it also makes me notice is that what is happening to kebab shops is what is happening to Chinese restaurants in the United States. Parents have been able to make enough of a crack in the class ceiling that they are newly able to send their kids to university, and make it so that these once intergenerational businesses have no one to be passed down to. Instead, they get sold or they shut. In the Australian context, they are on-sold to newer waves of migrants whose economic precarity matches what the Turkish community's once was: Syrians, Hazaras.

My mother doesn't read 'Meat' – we don't have that kind of relationship – although I seem to recall that I tell her about it because I am interviewed in a local newspaper on the topic, riding a little high off of my first small taste, really a morsel, of success. We are sitting next to one another at a cafe inside Blacktown Westpoint, which is a character unto itself in my psyche. The spectre that haunts my mental geography is this shopping centre. When I die I suspect that its interiors will be one of the few things that flashes before my eyes. I remember, anyway, my mother looking off speculatively, and making only one comment about 'Meat', which was to remark that I had gotten the nature of the labour wrong, or at least incomplete – that with my Berna character I had overlooked the large class of workers at these shops who are also highly educated, and in fact hold undergraduate and graduate qualifications that go unrecognised, or whose visa conditions prevent them from finding more appropriate, less depleting, work. 'It's just fiction,' I responded. These representations are necessarily partial. 'But you have a duty to get it right,' she said.

In April of 2020, thirty-year-old Burak Doğan was killed by a truck while on his bike, having just cancelled a trip from the food delivery service for which he worked. Burak had previously been employed as an industrial engineer in Turkey, arriving here to study English and earn a little money. The story made headlines because Burak continued to receive new delivery requests even as he lay dying, and furthermore, the company that had engaged his labour declined to recognise his death as a workplace fatality. The reason the company insurer refused to pay any compensation to Burak's family is because he died ten minutes after the insurance scheme's allotted fifteen-minute window of coverage following the completion or cancellation of an order. It was therefore unclear – legally, not morally – if he could have been considered on the clock or not. I find out that Burak died on Parramatta Road, only 150 metres away from my Petersham home, and his next of kin is the owner of a Turkish restaurant I patronise regularly. I was last there, physically, in 2019, before the pandemic, rolling in at midnight with two friends who ordered a kebab each. We stood on the kerb on the side of the road, dripping fresh onions and sauce and a kind of soggy lettuce juice everywhere, revelling.

I remember one final thing the publisher said, the one that I discussed my work with in 2018, back when I was still working on 'A Rock Is A Hard Place': that my work is about trauma, at its heart. 'And, if you think about it, migration is the originary trauma.' They compared my work to that of Judah Waten, author of *Alien Son,* a semi-fictionalised collection of stories about his family, which are communist in their outlook, or at least reflect, in their style and observations, the communist outlook of their author.

I'll spoil the meaning of my story, the one I wrote in 2016, because it's by no means a sleeper hit or a cult classic and you don't need to track it down and it doesn't really matter, except in the ways it matters to me. What I meant by 'Meat' is this: this country can eat you. It eats you. That's what my mother and father say, sometimes, exhaling at the end of a long day, my father perhaps peeling off his socks, crusted-on from the sweat of the work day, uncovering feet that smell, even from a distance, groaning audibly as he descends onto the couch, sighing in that particular way Turkish people do: with a little üff. Avustralya, yedin beni. Beni yedin hayat, bitirdin beni. Some of us eat; some of us are the meat.

*

'Simit getirdim,' I announce when I get back to the table. I drop the bag down and deposit our ayrans next to them, scattering some loose sesame seeds onto the plastic surface. We are trying the other kebab place this time, the one on Flushcombe Road that I like. The iskender comes out with large slices of fresh tomato on top, and we are liable to bump into almost no one we know here. From my vantage point I can watch the foot traffic moving in and out of one of Blacktown's many arcades, which, from childhood, has always housed a dry cleaner, a hair salon, a sari shop. 'İstersen dene.'

My mother looks up from her knitting, shedding little bits of wool onto the floor as she puts it back in her bag. She's very interested in her impending death these days. She regularly takes me through the contents of a large glory chest in which she has stored tens of pink and blue baby jumpers, totally unsuitable for the Australian climate, an intricately made pastel yellow blanket, layers and layers of crocheted tiny dresses and tea cosies. She likes to repeat 'Çeyizinize kalır artık' in response to my insufficiently expressed interest – in the chest and in having children to package into the clothing.

'Biz İzmirliler buna *gevrek* deriz.' She takes a tiny bite out of one. 'Bayat.' She puts it down.

*

Before they fell out, my mother's closest friend for a long time was a woman named Yonca. Her daughter and son were similar in age to myself and my sister Dilek, and I spent hundreds of hours of my youth at her homes in Berala and, later, Stanhope Gardens. When Yonca and her husband divorced, he moved to the Lake Macquarie region, fleeing debt and some angry Turkish men, and opened a kebab shop. My mother always called Yonca either *Kurnaz* or a *Çingene*, a racist way of noting her ability to stretch money pretty far, in contrast to my mother's approach – which I have, for better or worse, possibly inherited – of spending what one has. My mother often notes that the reason she never had more than a flat grand in her bank account for the duration of my youth is because of the generosity of her spirit. This is the aspect of her attitude to money that I try to emulate: the idea that money comes and money goes, and to cling to it too tightly suggests something negative about one's character. My father once remarked, 'What is money anyway? Put it in front of a dog and it wouldn't even sniff it'. I have to agree. My mother has always donated readily to any cause she is asked to, even by cold callers, has been sent in the mail multiple cheaply made, tiny seeing eye dogs that thank her for her charity, and sent several thousands of dollars to the needy in Turkey during Kurban Bayramı throughout her time here.

I liked Yonca, however, and am inclined to disagree with my mother's characterisation. When she felt in a certain mood, Yonca would rhapsodise about how cute she found us children, squeezing our cheeks till they hurt, calling me sarı papatya at a pitch and volume I despised, and calling my sister mor menekşe, marking our different colouring: me a little wan, my sister with dark hair and ceylan gözlü – deer eyes. At Yonca's home we ate ersatz kebabs – she routinely brought back home from her job boxes and boxes of pre-shaved meat left over at the end of the day, which we microwaved, watching with perverse interest the way that the frozen grease, white and solid, would thaw out, go translucent and drip pornographically. She would toast this for us in Lebanese bread, and then wrap it tightly in aluminium foil.

One summer our two families travelled to Coffs Harbour, staying at a caravan park near, I think, the Big Banana – a fact I recall only because I remember the way my sister and Yonca's two kids mocked me when I saw my first banana tree, somewhere on the premises of the Big Banana Fun Park, and wondered, out loud, 'Oh, do bananas grow on trees, do they?' They laughed and laughed, for days. Pardon me for remaining open to possibilities.

We visited the beach on that trip. I won't pretend to remember which one. All I do remember is all of us lying out on the sand, our towels laid out parallel to one another, and Yonca gazing up at a seagull flying overhead, squinting in a way that deepened the smile lines around her eyes, holding her hand up to her face to shade it, armpit hair on display. I had seen her fully in the nude hours before, by mistake – had wandered into her cabin while she was singing to herself, cooking us kids sucuklu yumurta for breakfast.

'Kuş olmak isterdim,' she said. Sighed, 'I wish I was a bird. I wish I could be a bird. Onların özgürlüğünü istiyorum.'

Second City

I spent the summer between 2013 and 2014, as many twenty-year-olds do, working at a restaurant. This one was on the corner of Church Street and Phillip Street, Parramatta. It was the type of place that opened at 7 am to welcome spandex-sporting cycling groups and old men with newspapers tucked under their arms, and closed as late in the evening as possible.

All staff members were expected to become all-rounders, equally capable of working the espresso machine, mixing cocktails, short-order cooking, taking orders on the floor or cashing out at the register, which was to say that we were all equally shit at everything, and so the food was systematically under- or over-cooked. Cups of coffee, when transported to a table, would slosh helplessly into saucers. This made us appear even less competent than we were. Few of us could coax a stabilising foam out of the old espresso machine, whose steaming wand was permanently encrusted with dried, old milk.

There was no air-conditioning to speak of, and as a career sweater I was frequently being advised to mop my upper lip by concerned workmates. Fortunately, the restaurant's main wall was composed of two folding glass doors, which we would push to the sides to let in some air, allowing customers to sit on couches facing the foot traffic and feel as if they were outside too. We had a fly problem that was so bad that customers demanded we close these doors to stop them coming in. I never knew how to tell them the flies came from inside.

Shifts were between ten and twelve hours long, and I could rarely convince anyone to take my spot on customer-facing floor duty, even though we were supposed to rotate. By the end of the day, I found it impossible to emote any longer. My facial muscles were locked in a rictus, the after-image of sustained smiling. For close, two of us would be left to clean up, only paid to work up to 12.30 am, but unlikely to knock off before 2; one of us would toss buckets of soapy water over the toilet floors and hope it knocked out some of the flies, while the other would wipe down food prep surfaces and tables in tight, furious circles, and then push them indoors; and then we would all but run home, stinking and with about six hours before we had to be back.

The wage was $17.49 an hour, no super, and at the end of each shift I would lie awake for hours, unable to sleep because my feet ached so badly. I hated working there and I was desperate to leave. I lasted four months. I was offered another job, selling wine in the Inner West, and quit.

My last night at the restaurant, it was March but still

sweltering. At midnight I was waiting for the last two customers to leave. When they called me over to the outside seating area, I said I regretted to inform them I couldn't offer them another round because we were closed. They happened to be Turkish, so the younger woman said to her friend, 'Ah! Ama ne güzel kafa çekiyorduk birlikte.'

I smiled, reminded of İstanbul, but remained firm, channelling a sort of desperate authoritarianism. I came very close to rising up and initiating my own one-person workers' revolution that night, but I was too tired to do anything except say goodbye to my compatriots. I went home and never came back.

I wrote some of these mundane details into short stories later: the kebab shop employee who has to rest her legs perpendicular up her wall so the swelling in her feet will come down; the young woman who sucks on olives while hidden in the kitchen in order to mainline herself enough salt and fat to make it through the day. It's important to represent the lived experiences of the working class.

I stopped working hospitality and retail in 2015, fortunate to crack into a white-collar position as a research assistant at my university. Instantly I was earning more than double what I used to make per hour. Because I credited the restaurant with my commie origin story, I felt ambivalent about this newfound class mobility – what it meant to step up and away from my roots, to instantly unlock an easier life for myself while others continued to struggle.

In 2017, I found myself back where I began, in Parramatta. I had decided to make a difference in my community through my new job: as a producer for a local literature organisation. The work felt like it was going to be important, and I felt like it had to be me who did it. All my life I had been a chubby, crooked-toothed, glasses-wearing nerd – not a self-declared nerd, either, and therefore the bad kind. I had been fortunate to discover literature at an early age, and spent most of my formative years at Max Webber Library or the Angus & Robertson in Blacktown Westpoint, accumulating a tiny empire of books which I buried myself into, to make up for my dearth of friends or much else.

My love of books and studying did open more material doors for me. For one, it threw me into the priority boarding lane of the 'Gifted and Talented' classes at Marayong Primary School. Such opportunities are made available arbitrarily, given that all eight-year-olds are much the same, but the die was cast. This leg-up got me into a selective high school, which then enabled me to study English literature and Spanish literature and post-colonial and Marxist theory at the University of Sydney, all of which had, by the year 2017, dyed my wool fully red.

On the other hand, though, wasn't I a sell-out? Surely I was placing distance between myself and regular people with all my sit-down jobs and book-learning, despite the fact that it was my supposedly cahil father who taught me the word capitalism, and which he meant as a pejorative.

I took great pains to remind myself that this literary work was radical in its own way. It was meaningful. Technically, it was the same work as anti-racism: there were young people of colour in Western Sydney, like me, who needed to be told that their stories were important and that they shouldn't be ashamed to tell them, that they could write and that they needn't stage their work in Parisian apartments or English meadows they had never visited. I was like a drunk at a bar buying everyone else a round, trying to share my good feeling, convinced that the sublime object which had liberated me – books and literature – could liberate everyone else too.

On my triumphant return to Parramatta, I was struck by all that had changed.

The graveyards of cigarette butts on the outdoor seating areas of Church Street were gone, thanks to the new smoke-free laws. When I had been working, we would tell customers in a low voice that while we couldn't supply them with ashtrays, we could sneak them take-away piccolo-size coffee cups filled with a little water to butt into. More than half of the hookah joints had been forced to shut their doors for this reason. In their place stood familiar Inner West and Inner City institutions: Bourke St Bakery, Jamie's Italian, Gelato Messina. The famous Hungry Jack's building, which was the site of stabbings, drug deals and cheeky chunders, which was closed down in 2013, had now been ripped away, along with the old library where I had previously spent hundreds of hours tutoring high schoolers (another example of my early fixation on transmitting the Power of Knowledge). These mainstays had been cleared to make room for the linkage between Parramatta Square and the Parramatta River foreshore, which was set to beautify and elevate the area, and render it more habitable to wholesome families and public servants.

Even the Roxy, Parramatta's most iconic building, had been left functionless. Although it was long notable for being a little sketchy, the building was pristine in my eyes: clean vertical lines in white, touches of red tile, a sumptuous quantity of rounded archways. Perturbed, and shuffling now down the street with my head buried in my phone, I pulled up an article announcing that the Roxy would soon be transformed into an office tower. Restaurants, cafes and shops at ground level, the original facade, and a hulking spire of glass offices built up on top, and liable to send Fredric Jameson into a tailspin.

Parramatta was well on its way to becoming Sydney's 'Second City'. Several government offices had made the move for the cheaper rent, and the transition to high-rises was going strong. All along the river new housing was being built, boutique hotels as well as serviced apartments. Western Sydney University's Parramatta campus had been erected, as if overnight, while I was gone, and its red logo drew the eye like a laser pointer. When I started attending workshops at nearby high schools, the students of a local school had been moved to a temporary campus, and were being taught out of demountables connected by wobbly, plastic ramps, which, a teacher informed me, had been thrown up in two months. The school was set to reopen as a high-rise. One of the students isn't taking it well, she remarked. He likes to go outside and let his feet touch the ground on occasion, feel the grass – it helps him think.

Still, it felt a little nice, too. The next day, I rolled in at

8 am. I was running early to meet a writing mentor. To kill time, I grabbed a muffin and a coffee from Bourke St Bakery, quite chuffed that the influx of bourgeois taste had finally brought in the type of latte I was used to sipping in the Inner West – soy, with a floret on top to boot, something I had never quite learned to make myself, and which altered nothing about the experience except the symbolic. The addition of latte art suggested care and value, for me and my impressive feat of owning four dollars. Latte-sipping is over-saturated as a metonym of ridicule by now, but I do believe it has something potent to say about the passage I had completed through the velvet ropes of labour relations. Debord described such a transition in his 1967 *The Society of the Spectacle*:

> once [their] workday is over, the worker is …
> redeemed from the total contempt toward them that
> is so clearly implied by every aspect of the organisation
> and surveillance of production, and finds themselves
> seemingly treated like a grownup, with a great show of
> politeness, in his new role as a consumer.

I lazed like a veritable bon vivant on one of the new, brightly painted benches, which faced the water feature in the centre of Parramatta Square, watched pedestrians pass, most of them in dress shirts and pencil skirts. Outside the Town Hall the council had placed a ping-pong table, and I observed a beefy tradie in yellow high-vis playing against a short, older man in a puffy vest. What a multicultural utopia, I thought, putting out my foot to halt the ping-pong ball on its roll away from the players.

Wandering down the streets of Parramatta or Harris Park now, it is hard not to be lulled into a temporary state of safety and respectability. The night lives of these suburbs – supposedly – have been newly reoriented around sitting down to a $25 meal at six, chucking back a handful of mukhwas at eight, and returning home and to bed by nine, rather than the fantasies the *Daily Telegraph* might previously have had us entertain about being carjacked or finding oneself in a punch-on.

Still, and mukhwas notwithstanding, people like me have been conditioned to recognise gentrification as a social harm. Something enacted by right-wing governments and the white middle class who need to step out of their hemp outfits and then go straight to getting fucked. We are agreed that we should do all we can to end its effects, and puzzle over how to invite economic development into an area without displacing, or replacing, its existing populace. Governments and activists have experimented with policies geared at achieving this, advocating for zoning controls, taxation incentives and affordable housing minimums that can preserve the social and ethnic make-up of an area.

In Parramatta, anti-gentrification proponents have been focused on halting the arrival of light rail, as well as expanding the North Parramatta heritage precinct, advocating for the preservation of various terrace houses and villas, as well as Parramatta Gaol, and the Parramatta Female

Factory – settlement-era buildings said to capture vital parts of Parramatta's working-class history. This activism is in the vein of that conducted by individuals such as Juanita Nielsen in Potts Point in the seventies, aimed at preventing workers' cottages and single-storey terrace houses from being torn down and replaced by high-density housing for the upper classes. These North Parramatta buildings have taken their place alongside other imperial jewels: Elizabeth Farm, the Macquarie Gate House, the suburb's churches, the Lancer Barracks, and Old Government House; Parramatta's cultural touchstones.

I wondered if there was a way for the arts sector to fight one of the battles of the anti-gentrification war. The mission statement of independent American publisher, Akashic Books, for example, is to 'reverse-gentrify' US literature. It was possible, I thought, to do something with the burgeoning sums of money that had been allocated to the arts in Parramatta. Western Sydney has been in recent years designated a 'priority area' for government arts funding, both as an election tactic and for the arts' supposed crime and violence prevention benefits. The reasoning is that if young people have a place to go at night, or if a city has a vibrant night life, then the streets become safer to walk after dark and youths have something to do other than jack cars or drink on stoops. Young, brown, Muslim men in particular are viewed, from a policy perspective, as being able to be deradicalised if they are deferred from mosques over to music, sport, theatre. This link that has emerged between countering violent extremism initiatives and the funding of the arts in Western Sydney – which should be funded regardless of its national security implications – makes the arts a part of the police-industrial complex, and all of us harmless cardigan-wearing bespectacled arts workers technically cops. Still, people like me could ensure that such funding went towards improving skills and opportunities for the people who already lived here, and who genuinely needed it.

After my fourth months as a Parramatta arts worker, it was difficult to avoid the reality that, for the most part, the individuals who were finding our public events and opportunities were not those I had imagined. A great many already possessed certain resources. Free time. An a priori level of wealth that made them entertain the idea that they could legitimately pursue writing for themselves or their children. The knowledge of how to look these things up; or the sense of possibility required to believe that there was anything to look up. Unfortunately, although our costs were pegged as low we could manage, several locals nonetheless advised us that they couldn't afford our programs.

And I should have known this; it's not as if I had written any optional words between the years 2010 and 2015, not as if I had attended any workshops or readings. I was busy, trying not to cark it, tunnel-visioning via the strength of my focus on just surviving and then thriving, working my way into a comfortable position in life through brute force. Only after that had the words burbled up.

As an under-resourced and understaffed organisation, it was easier to go where we knew there was need than to manufacture demand. Many of the students we engaged with our public programs were children of colour, of course, and very cute – in our office we had hung up an artwork entitled *Ways of Saying Hello*, with community language greetings contributed by a group of kid workshop participants, which read Salaam, Talofa, Vanakkam, Nǐhǎo – and I enjoyed watching them develop pride and confidence in their budding voices. But, equally, they were often part of families who planned to also send their kids to tutoring colleges, or wanted them to engage in literature to improve their prospects of securing university entry. The children of parents who read to their kids because one of them could afford not to work – or because they could read, in English or at all.

We in the literary community are often guilty of romanticising the plights and output of decorated writers who mop floors, like Enrique Ferrari, an Argentinian novelist who is a metro janitor in Buenos Aires by day, or who clean buildings, like Caitriona Lally, who made headlines when she won the Rooney Prize for Irish Literature in 2018. She was awarded the prize by Trinity College Dublin, the same university where she worked as a cleaner. I think it is more important not to impute bootstrapping narratives onto the stories of people like myself or others fighting worse structural oppressions, who make writing or the arts work by cleaning toilets or mixing drinks. We represent overwhelming exceptions to Virginia Woolf's observation that 'one cannot think well, love well, sleep well, if one has not dined well'. Possession of the means to write is strong evidence of, on average, a not-quite-proletarian status.

Parramatta, though, has been home to a significant middle class, immigrant or not – not always, but for a good long while. Certainly the area has long been derided by the intelligentsia and elites for its supposedly elevated crime rate, its lack of social and cultural facilities, and for its preponderance of brown and black folk and public housing. However, Sydney's western suburbs have also been zones of affluence and comfort for settlers. Post-war Coalition and Labor governments sponsored home ownership in Western Sydney, and facilitated the mass construction of homes with backyard pools and barbecues and Hills Hoists. As Michael Bounds and Alan Morris note, securing 'the detached home in suburbia was the backbone of the Australian dream', and the Australian dream is inextricable from the colonisation of this continent. Any account of the evil of gentrification in Parramatta which overlooks the original root of that evil, colonisation, is doomed, therefore, to remain either ahistorical or apolitical.

*

Parramatta has often felt like home ground to me – fifteen minutes on the train from where I grew up in Blacktown, and so a prime spot for shopping, socialising, picnics and nights out. For over a decade, sitting beside my father in his ute, driving from Blacktown to Parramatta to Auburn – Sydney's Turkish diasporic centre – on our way to purchase something from a specialty grocer or sweets store, he would point out the occasional house, his eyes flickering for a moment before returning to the road.

'Bak.' I would dutifully swivel my head. 'O evi ben yaptım.'

I would facetiously give the requisite 'Wow', remark on the straightness of the bricks, and ask questions designed to draw out choice anecdotes he wanted to tell about homes he had helped build. But I did genuinely feel a little buoyed. We had made our mark upon these parts, our family, having made the migration in the eighties poor, and building ourselves up, brick by brick.

In Europe, primarily France and Germany, countries which have significant diasporic populations, one of the foremost racist stereotypes that exists about Turks is that we make reliable builders, and good bosseurs. Unlike other Middle Easterners, Turks aren't lazy, but rather work hard, running kebab shops or engaging in masonry. It's part pat on the head, part slap in the face, given that Turks rebuilt a destroyed Germany after the war. Their labour was imported en masse through guest worker programs, with the end goal of booting everyone back out when all was done. Turks were viewed as an unassimilable population, due to their status as Muslims, and as such needed to be permanently denied avenues to citizenship and sent back to where they came from. The status of Turks as builders and 'hard workers' in Europe, therefore, tends to denote their status as perpetual other, a domestic alien or kanak, and signifies their permanent assignation to the working class – tireless creators of homes for a nation which does not want the builders of those homes to ever live in one themselves.

But Western Europe is not Australia. Here, people like my father and me have built on top of other things, directly and violently. As Randa Abdel-Fattah has written, Turks were the first Muslims to be allowed to immigrate into Australia under post-war migration, in 1967, and have endured racism and Islamophobia since. However, the relaxation of Australia's immigration policies, which allowed increasing amounts of olive to brown migration and naturalisation at relatively high rates, has much to do with the state's populate or perish policy, and the desire to settle vast territories stolen from Aboriginal populations more efficiently. Although the Australian suburban identity is today inextricable from whiteness, immigrant labour created the conditions of its possibility.

One of my final acts as a Parramatta arts producer was to compile the research for an app the organisation developed, geared at encouraging on-foot exploration of the suburb and greater engagement with its history and culture. I tracked down archival photographs, pieced together whimsical historical anecdotes about ghosts and windmills, visited and revisited the Parramatta Heritage Centre, and then took tens of kilometres of walks in order to triangulate the spots I wanted to include.

Finally, I found myself stopped in the middle of Parramatta Park, feet blistered and aching from my office sandals. I stood holding up a piece of paper I had printed out from a study documenting the various trees in the park, some of which still bore visible 'scars'. These were markings from sections of the tree which had had their bark stripped away by the Burramatta people of the Dharug nation, to build canoes. I was mind-fucked by the reminder of how recently colonisation began in what we currently call Australia.

I left this job soon after. Of course, my experiences there are only emblematic of the underlying, structural issues which impact the entire arts sector, and for which no individual organisation is culpable. I am grateful it encouraged me to take a longer view on the gentrification of the suburb. It helped to stop riling me that Parramatta was to become a 'Second City', bringing in out-of-towners who had no idea what it was like to grow up in the area, to live through the racism or the terrible hospital waits, or to know all the Turkish restaurant owners by name. Or, it did continue to rile me, but my reasons changed.

Parramatta was New South Wales's first central business district, not its second, as it was the stronger of the two trade and agricultural hubs before businesses drifted back up-river. With these changes, Parramatta is only reclaiming a status it once already held. Likewise, the arrival of light rail to the area will signify a return; what used to be an extensive tramway was only ripped up in the sixties. It is impossible to form a politically and historically satisfying account of gentrification in Parramatta without going all the way back, and recognising that Parramatta was first, very first, a Blak centre, a meeting place bearing economic, cultural and spiritual significance for the aforementioned people of the Dharug nations.

What, then, do I make of current anti-gentrification movements in Parramatta, with their focus on preserving colonial buildings? If continual displacement of local populations in the name of 'development' is Parramatta's story, and if displacement did not begin five years ago but 230 years ago, what use is there in attempting to freeze its current class and racial composition in amber?

Recognising these tensions goes a long way to identifying the light stink of white supremacy that underpins many urban conservation projects today. Although it is a truism, it is worth underscoring the point that heritage and conservation projects are, in point of fact, conservative. As is clear in the current challenges being faced in having the Brewarrina Fish Traps, one of the oldest human-made structures on earth, World Heritage–listed, or preventing a go-cart track being constructed on Wahluu, what is considered heritage and what is worth conserving are determined by the powerful. Indeed, 'defending our heritage' is a phrase that sits easily in a white supremacist lexicon, and the sites that have been deemed most worthy of protection in Parramatta today bespeak a colonial nostalgia.

Any attempt to restore places like Parramatta from middle-class and white clutches back over to multicultural ones, and to its suburban origins, represents an attempt to reclaim what does not belong to us. The un-gentrification of Parramatta, then, if it is taken far enough, if it is to host a truly radical impulse, is perhaps better called, simply, decolonisation.

To conclude this essay, then, I would like to offer some reflections on what a decolonised Parramatta could look like. I mean to use the word in the least symbolic, figurative, or metaphorical sense possible, but at the same time prefer to remain epistemologically humble. If I thought I knew anything about anything, perhaps I would fare better at holding down a job.

First, I would caution against buying into a discourse about winding back the clock to a pristine past. Such navel-gazing does little for the present, and neglects the persistence of neo-colonial practices of displacement affecting Aboriginal communities right this very second. Indeed, two Indigenous-led 'anti-gentrification' movements, whose aims are better dubbed as decolonial, and merit greater attention, concern the Parramatta Girls Home and the Block at Redfern.

Second, I would note that decolonising approaches both to our suburbs and our literature require a more radical approach than the twin mirages of policy reform or symbolic activity. None of this is to undermine the value of symbolic empowerment, or the meaningfulness of self-representation. Only to emphasise the fact that these activities must run alongside material approaches, starting with support for treaty, return of land, and reparations.

Otherwise we have no hope of uplifting more than lucky, upwardly mobile individuals who remain that way, forever individualised, without access to a community. To raise the class status of one person is to create more members of the middle class, piled on top of others less privileged. However, to raise the class status of an entire class is to abolish class. And that doesn't happen with words, as much as I wish that were the case, for this hobby of mine would feel like less of a hobby and more of a life purpose if that were true. Wealth, land, and the means of production, just as much in literature as anywhere else, require radical redistribution. In the words of poet Alison Whittaker, 'what I'm looking for is wealth transfer – I'm looking for a shift in the conversation that puts feet on the ground and food on the table.'

Rahat

That there is no easy or comfortable translation for 'awkward' in other languages suggests that I'm only myself in English. This feels like a loss, because I'd like to think of myself as Turkish, too. An internet search on this subject – is awkwardness an Anglophone phenomenon? – will throw up near-miss translations, foreign words that instead capture strangeness, discomfort, ugliness, untidiness, clumsiness. Some languages have resorted to borrowing the word from English wholesale – Spanish and German use 'awkward' the way they use 'download' or 'spinning'. In Turkish we say tuhaf or sakar. One means strange, the other clumsy.

When I am young, I go through a phase of falling down all the time and scraping my knee.

'This is why you need to always hold my hand,' says my mother, grabbing it into hers as the pedestrian stoplight flicks to green and we cross the road on our walk home from school. 'Your abla held my hand until she was fourteen. It's perfectly normal back home.'

My nickname for a long time ends up being Sakar Şakir, after the Kemal Sunal character.

*

In Spain, I pick a flat in barrio Begoña. I am meant to go and inspect several housing options, and select the one I like most – as normal people do – but in the end I only see one. I haven't slept for the six days I've been in Madrid so far. I've been staying at a hostel on the Gran Vía, and I'm afraid every night, for no reason, that someone will kick the door down. Or that I will never find a place to live and I'll run through my savings living out of an Airbnb. Or I'll lose my scholarship, which is paying for me to be here; or I'll lose my mind.

In my hostel room, I have been barricading myself in by wedging my suitcase against the door at night, with its handle up. I have brought with me a rubber doorstop which I bought from Bunnings back home, and I secure my door that way sometimes too. I think of a loved one sleeping with a knife under their pillow, at age fourteen and again at forty. I think that my symptom is their symptom.

Stepping into daylight, up and out of the metro station at Begoña, I check my watch and notice the inspection is scheduled for ten minutes from now, but the phenomenon of 'Spanish time', which I am still familiarising myself with, suggests I have another half hour to wait. There's a Mercadona en route so I head in to pass the minutes, soothed by the familiar format of the supermarket, and the predictable, repetitive jingle that sings out the store's name.

I am obsessed, during this period, with fibre. If I don't get enough of it something will go wrong or I'll surely die, so I pull out a bottle of orange juice that I assume comes with pulp – 'pulpa' is an obvious equivalent for the English word. I'll add my own flaxseed to it later, to turn it into a dense, gummy mixture that I find fibrous enough.

The bottle goes into my backpack but I don't end up ever drinking it; my prospective roommate appears out the front of the flat and the inspection goes by in a rush. I say I'll rent it on the spot, even though it's thirty minutes out of the city, there is no lock for the bedroom door, and I am supposed to inspect another place in an hour. I am too anxious about resolving this need for housing as quickly as possible, and I don't want to meet an unending bevy of strangers.

I live with a woman named Martina in Madrid's barrio Begoña for six months, and the whole time she speaks to me in unrelenting, rapid Spanish I can barely understand, in part because her accent is from the south. The night I move in, before she realises I am not who she wishes I was, she takes me out dancing with her Latin American friends – two from Mexico, two from Honduras. She says she can only be friends with Latin Americans because the Spaniards from the centre and the north are too cold, not like southerners, warm and friendly.

We stand in a crowded bar and eat potato chips and bland tapas, and they dance salsa until almost sunrise the next day, soft-shoeing around shards of broken glass and sticky floor patches.

'I'm not a good dancer,' I insist, trying to stay seated and make myself heard over the din, in accented Spanish, but one of them, Ivan, pulls me up anyway. He leads, spinning me to and fro with so much force I lose control of my body.

*

I have been out salsa dancing only one other time: the year before I left for exchange, with a loved one.

At Oxford Art Factory I stare at an artwork they have mounted on the wall, a rendering of Rihanna's face as it appeared in the police report after Chris Brown assaulted her, as the music pumps. I feel too awkward to dance and give my loved one a good time. She stands next to me, as I sit prone on my bar stool, and moves her body forwards and backwards, doing the right motions.

We leave around nine, after we spot a man that she used to date, before. He's with his long-term girlfriend, twirling her easily on the dance floor, and they're looking at each other, almost cheek to cheek, and laughing.

'We should leave,' she says. She slips on her red jacket, worn to match the occasion. 'Besides, you're not even fucking dancing.'

During that first month in the flat with Martina, in a last-ditch attempt to impress her, I bring over Elise, a friend I have somehow made. She is Belgian, speaks five languages and chats easily. Elise and Martina get along well, stand beside each other near the stove and grill vegetables. After she leaves, Martina comments that she really likes Elise.

'She's not like you at all,' she says.

After that, I stay hidden in my bedroom until Martina

leaves the house, at 7.40 every morning, to go to the gym for spin class. Only after the front door slams shut do I creep out of my room, feeling guilty.

*

My father buys my eldest sister Gülin, his step-daughter, flowers, in 1994. He has them sent to her work, her first office job out of university, based in North Sydney. The flowers scare her.

I listen to a podcast about a prisoner about to get out who spends a long time thinking about the choreography of a hug – does only one arm go up and over, or both arms over? One time I practise something similar with a friend, Melanie, who hugs me often. She loops her arm into my mine without hesitation whenever we walk side by side, or takes my hand in hers and swings them, clasped. Melanie is easily affectionate, and doesn't care that everyone in the high school thinks we're dating. Maybe we are – I can't tell. She has these black curls that catch the light and shine; when we hug, her hair always smells strong and floral, freshly washed. I think that I hate to hug because I hate to shower; later I realise I don't shower so I have a reason not to hug.

After the HSC, Melanie teaches me how to ride a bike; she has me go down Rotaract Hill, behind Seven Hills station, over and over again, as trains roar by, until I can balance with ease, and then she starts me pedalling.

My father places a coin into my palm like I'm diseased, dropping it and withdrawing, taking care not to let our skin touch. My father and I have, to my memory, never hugged.

Too many men, other men, have made the idea of doing so seem either verboten or simply too awkward to try now.

*

I walk out of my bedroom one day, and my partner is sitting on the chair by the door where we put on our shoes, wedging his foot into one of his brown boots. I let out a low scream.

'Um, sorry,' I say, when I realise it's Justin. I mislocated him in space – thought he was in some other part of the house. We hug goodbye. During, I notice I have finally stopped thinking about the choreography of hugs.

*

I joke about having a 'thicc amygdala', but in reality I do, and I want to shrink her. I comfort her often, telling her I appreciate what she's doing for me – that even though I know she's only trying to protect me, I don't need her right now. No psychologist outside of a podcast has told me to approach my anxiety in this manner, but I do it anyway.

The only psychologist who ever comments on whether my hypervigilance is appropriate says, 'What have you got to be anxious about?' and 'It's funny, the way you describe your symptoms sounds like PTSD.'

Of course I stop seeing her. She's not wrong; there is nothing to be anxious about, which is what qualifies a regular emotion as a disorder.

My current psychologist, in a similar vein, says, 'Australia is a doddle, isn't it?'

It's a British word – she means, it's easy to live here.

You're safe ninety-nine percent of the time. I start to tell my amygdala that too: *Australia is a doddle.* I tell my amygdala that she doesn't need to ape others, people who are in perpetual crisis, and whose fear is well-earned.

After the session, we sit over this psychologist's EFTPOS machine and take turns punching in numbers and alternating swipes of my Medicare card and debit card. She tends to continue our sessions all the way through this process, so she asks, 'Nothing like this has ever happened to you, though, right?' We spend most of our session discussing my family's traumas as if they were my own.

'No.'

*

My mother and I share an elevator in Blacktown shopping centre, riding up to level three. She reaches past me to press the button and I flinch. She rears back like I scalded her.

'What's wrong with you?' she says. Her eyes flash. 'Who abused *you?*'

*

I see a meme on Twitter that diaspora kids go mad for. About the way second-generation POC love to hide in their bedrooms when friends of the family come by. It's funny because it's true.

As a child, I do it because I can never quite figure out how I am supposed to pull off naturally kissing someone on their cheeks – these things take concentration, deliberation and effort, like visualising how you might land a plane. And if it is a man, do I still do it? Or do we only grasp hands? If they extend their hand, am I supposed to kiss it and press it to my forehead? Is that only during some times of the year? How old is too old to do the forehead-press?

When I am seven, in Üçkuyular, my grandmother is dying of hepatitis C. I don't know her – we have only met once, and then this second time, when my mother wheels her out into the hospital lobby. She is wearing a pastel pink hospital gown and her stomach is distended; she looks pregnant despite being seventy-seven. We shake hands, something formal and unnatural. She can't kiss me because her hepatitis is contagious; she herself contracted it in her youth, taking care of a dying neighbour in Tire, cleaning up the woman's shit and all, because the neighbour's husband wouldn't.

My mother spends all of her time at the hospital, so myself and my older sister Dilek, who is eleven, pass through the hands of my mother's myriad female friends, who step in without having to be asked. They come by my grandmother's flat every second day with meals, take us out to play with the neighbourhood kids, squeeze our chubby cheeks and call us easy endearments like tatlım and şekerim. My mother's brother Murat takes us a couple of times, walking us to the bakkal where he buys us Eti Pufs and Çokokrem and damla sakızı. He teaches and forces us to rehearse a routine in which we alternate sitting and standing, and each have to chant:

'En büyük Beşiktaş!'

'Başka büyük yok!'

Louder.

'En büyük Beşiktaş!'

'Başka büyük yok!'

I overhear my mother talking about Murat and us with my abla, in low voices, a snatch of the word alkol. Or I think I do – I don't know how I know it's not safe to be alone with him after that, but I do know. Our supply of sweets dries up; when we see him he's not impressed, acts distracted, cold, even if we try to make him smile by repeating the routine.

*

My desire to hide foments my reputation inside the Turkish community as being a little bit of a stuck-up, assimilated bookworm. The effect is doubled when my mother starts to lean into the explanation to excuse my behaviour. *She's studying. She has a test.* These are impermeable excuses inside a culture which prizes the upwardly mobile. *Oh, she's going to save us all. She's going to do us all so proud. A test. We should leave her in peace.*

If family friends spill into the room I am secured in, I try to act as if I was, the whole time, just on my way out to join them.

'No, no,' they say. 'Don't worry, you keep studying. I'll prepare the food.'

If they inquire about why I'm not out on the frontline, working the lounge room, distributing squirts of kolonya or chocolates out of the sugar bowl into waiting hands, my mother starts to add, *She's very clumsy.*

A family friend named Ayten is at my parent's house when I am visiting. She is famous for her Turkish coffee, and offers to show me how to prepare it just right. My mother offers me up as a joke, knowing I will never be the ev kızı or an evde kalmış kız; that ship has sailed, because I have lived out of home, unwed, since I was nineteen.

I stand, awkwardly, next to Ayten by the stove, as she brings a cezve up to a near-boil.

'Köpürsün ama kaynamamalı,' she says. 'Oradan fincan getirir misin?'

I go and retrieve the small cups and hand her one. She pours, places it down, holds out her hand for the next cup, and I start to dole them out in a rhythm.

'Her bardağın köpük ölçüsü aynı olmalı,' she explains, raising one cup and pouring its contents into another, redistributing the foam so they all match.

'Tamam,' I say. 'Harika.' Ayten is only fluent in Turkish, but I want to limit my speech around her so she doesn't notice my accent. She mistakes my brevity for disinterest.

'I know, I'm being so pedantic, aren't I?' She looks at me sidelong. 'It's like, the same way people probably like to take really good care at a real job, you know. You probably prepare your files or notes in a really rigorous way ... it's like that.'

*

I start a PhD, and am shocked by the latitude I am given to read whatever texts I want whenever I want, and call it research. I mill through Chomsky's back catalogue, although he is only tenuously relevant to my work. He writes, 'There has been a conscious effort to atomise the society for a long time, to break people up, to break down what are called secondary associations in the sociological literature:

groups that interact and construct spaces in which people can formulate ideas, test them, begin to understand human relations and learn what it means to cooperate with each other. Unions were one of the major examples of this, and that's part of the reason for their generally very progressive impact on society. And, of course, they've been a major target of attack, I think, partially for that reason. The whole concept of social solidarity is considered very threatening by concentrated power.'

It's late by the time I take a break – it's gone dark all around me, but I hadn't noticed, had escaped self-awareness for a few hours with my head in a book – so I order something off Menulog. The wait generates anxiety.

I put on a bra – mostly as a prop, in order to temporarily perform decency to the delivery driver – well before the guy shows up. He passes me my meal and I go back to my book. For a crazed half-second before the interaction passes, I think to myself, the worst thing that could possibly ever happen is if this guy tried to talk to me right now.

*

I spend days at a time at home without seeing anyone except Justin in the evenings; there's no reason to leave the house as a postgraduate student. There are few work spaces on campus, my formal supervision requirements rarely need my physical presence on campus, and all of our work is done by and for ourselves. I reason that it's thrifty to stay at home – if I go out to a cafe, or wear and have to wash or buy clean clothes, I lose money. I'd rather lose my mind.

Mark Fisher writes, 'Anxiety is the emotional state that correlates with the (economic, social, existential) precariousness which neoliberal governance has normalised.'

When I finally go out, I do so with my earphones in to dull the ambient noise of traffic, and powerwalk down Crystal Street. It feels strange, navigating without being able to zoom in or rotate it like you can on Google Maps. This feeling is the same feeling as dissociation.

I walk to the cafe by Petersham Park. I listen to my podcast psychologist discuss '5 Ways Technology Is Making Us Anxious'. Dr Ellen Hendriksen explains that one of the effects of smartphones, and push notifications in particular, is to create a (false) sense of alarm and urgency, a constant anticipation that an alert could go off at any moment, with no predictability. A second, linked, phenomenon is that technology feeds anxiety by enabling us not to talk to one another – instead of asking for directions we can pull up a map, for example – and so erodes our tolerance for human interaction, and unpredictability, and prevents us from building social ease.

When I order my coffee, I can't make eye contact with the barista because it doesn't feel natural yet – I can't stop thinking about my face, what it is doing or failing to do, or if my voice, my accent, sound correct like everyone else's.

While I wait I read a tweet: 'just did my shortest uber delivery: the dude was standing OUTSIDE the restaurant and just paid me to go in and pick up his burger so he didnt have to speak to the workers ???' I hit *like*.

*

Simply because a language lacks a vocabulary for talking about social anxiety and awkwardness doesn't mean it doesn't exist. The Sapir-Whorf hypothesis, which says that the language a person speaks can determine how they see the world – for example, a language that lacks the word for *blue* bars its speakers from perceiving the colour – has some applications, but it cannot reliably pump out confident, charismatic individuals who don't suffer from shyness. All it does is invisibilise them.

In 1987, my eldest sister, her step-father – my father – and my mother move to Sydney. Within a few years my father has started his own bricklaying business. The first time he ever has to pay taxes for himself, he books in to see an accountant with my sister's help. It's before I am born but my sister tells me that that day my father comes out of his bedroom in a dress shirt, shaven and smelling like cologne.

'His hands just would not stop shaking.' My sister rolls her eyes. 'He was that nervous about meeting some random guy.'

*

Another meme on Twitter that millennials like to share. It's about phone anxiety – that under no circumstances is anyone allowed to call us. Even if the world is ending, you should just text. I feel it deeply when I first start working at a women's domestic violence service in 2016. Justin recommends it to me as a way to direct all my energy about gender and violence and abuse. The service is entirely phone-based; the two social workers I am interning for make two or three hundred phone calls a day, offering women, who are referred to us by the police, access to counselling and other services. A few weeks in, the social workers are so swamped they have to let me have a crack on phones; so far I have only been doing admin, preparing files and punching holes.

'Write yourself a script if you need to,' Sarah says. 'Let me know how you go.' She turns back to her computer and that's the extent of the hand-holding I receive.

I psych myself up by telling myself it's better to be on this end of the call, to goad or guilt myself into being a useful member of society. I do write a script, with a shaky hand, and I read off it. Eventually I don't need one anymore and it starts to come naturally. Like Elise, I even start to record long, rambling voice memos that I send to friends when I don't have the energy to text.

'Don't you hate the sound of your own voice, though?' one asks, finding the practice strange.

'Of course I hate the sound of my own voice,' I respond. 'Who doesn't hate the sound of their own voice?'

*

My phone confidence only grows after I work an office job in the arts. My co-worker and immediate supervisor has lived in London for a decade and worked in children's television programming in two countries. Her personality is effortless warmth. During school holidays, she brings her two young kids into the office, and throughout the day they come up to offer her slow, long hugs from behind. Her tone is always calm, no matter if they misbehave, scribble over all the paper in our printer. The way she forms the letter *s* is sibilant – it comes out almost like a whistle. After a few months, I notice I start doing it too.

*

In 2017, my mother, father and I catch the train to Redfern station and start the walk up to the university. I had finished my undergraduate studies the year before, but the graduation takes place the following May. I sweat onto my white dress, and it starts to drip down my pits and tickle its way down the sides of my torso.

I collect my cap and gown while my parents wait outside nearby. I am relieved to be shrouded in the heavy black fabric.

When I emerge, my father is nowhere to be seen.

'Babam nerede?' I say, and take a seat beside my mother on the brown bench outside the toilet. She is waiting for my father to return so he can give her some cash to buy me a stuffed graduation bear, although I insist I don't want or need one. She is angry that she and my father have come to my graduation empty-handed, now that she has observed other students clasping great bunches of flowers to their chests, or are sashaying about, easily swinging bottles of champagne and plastic glasses from their arms.

She jerks her thumb at the bathrooms.

'On beş dakikada bir tuvalete gidiyor bugün. Mutlaka bir rahatsızlığı var.' She starts to cry, convinced he has some physical health condition he has been hiding from the family, and which is manifesting in frequent bathroom visits today.

'Or he's just anxious,' I say. She dries up – I have always marvelled at the way she starts and stops crying on a dime, and am thankful I have managed to cultivate better emotional regulation throughout the years – and starts to nod in thought.

When my father emerges from the bathroom, wiping his hands down his dress pants, she says, 'Neyin var senin? What the fuck is wrong with you? Eda needs a fucking bear.'

*

I start leaving the house every day because my psychologist insists. On the long walk from Petersham to uni, down Parramatta Road, I watch YouTube videos, staring down into my phone turned up to full brightness. I find them soothingly optional. They're the mental equivalent of having your hair stroked; you could or could not choose to pay attention, take or leave the stimulus. I watch a video essay about *The Big Bang Theory*, a show I have never watched. The *Pop Culture Detective* points out that wealthy white men are rarely punished for being socially anxious, or disregarding social mores. Instead, they are dubbed misunderstood geniuses.

*

Dilek, whom I have never been able to refer to as abla because our age difference is only four years, schedules her wedding for two days after I return from Spain. Naturally, there is bedlam when I arrive; the DJ has dropped out last minute, and the Greek side of the groom's family want a bouzouki player to perform instead, an idea my mother can't stand. In addition, my sister has no one lined up on her side to speak. Not a single speech to speak of. Abla and my mother and my father all dig in their heels and refuse, each of them insisting that they're the one who is least comfortable speaking in front of a crowd.

'Please,' says my sister. She looks gaunt, with dark circles under her eyes. She has lost weight from the stress of planning the wedding. 'You're the nerdy one. And you have good English. You can write a speech easy.'

The time away has made me calmer; I notice it about myself, the way my head doesn't heat up and I never shake or lose control of the volume of my voice anymore. I write and deliver a speech. It pleases my sister, which pleases me.

*

My father carefully organises his life so that he can run a business by word of mouth. All of his referrals come through the extensive network of Turks and other wogs in Western Sydney, and if you need him you call him or he calls you. His phone is hooked to his pants at all times. I send him Facebook messages to which he does not respond.

For my sister's most recent birthday, my mother gets it in her head that he should make a contribution to the card in his own hand, for once. She deploys me to cajole him out of the backyard, where he spends hours roaming up and down his rows of plants, disturbing them obsessively with the tip of a shovel, or turning their leaves over in his hand to inspect their undersides for insects. This time, I think he has gone there to hide.

'Seni kırmaz,' says my mother. 'He'll do it if you ask him to.'

I wave my father over and sit him down in a chair on the patio. When he notices he's cornered, he says, jokingly, 'Ama ben okuma yazma bilmiyorum.'

Placing the card open in front of him, I lay down my phone next to it. On it, I have pulled up an image which reads, 'Happy Birthday and Best Wishes to my Daughter. I love you.'

'Kopya çek,' I say, thinking it will make it easier, and he copies out the letters. I make sure to look away so I can't see his hand shake.

*

When my father loses his driver's licence, it is a long time coming. He resents following these nanny-state road rules, and in particular the one regarding his seatbelt; he thinks they're less safe than going without, all because he once jumped from the driver's side to the passenger seat when he got t-boned, emerging from what would have otherwise been a fatal encounter unscathed. He won't accept criticism of the way he drives a car because, he insists, none of us know what we're talking about, although I do eventually earn my licence in 2020.

My father continues to take jobs, despite his suspension. As the sole income provider for my mother and himself, he is unable to take six months off work, and prefers to risk imprisonment than take money from me. I post an ad up on Gumtree for a driver – anyone at all who is willing to chauffeur him, in his ute, to these work sites. The ad receives eleven responses, and I text with them diligently, impersonating my father, directing them to his house, and my father meets them all.

*

For shits and giggles, because we have a stray ten minutes, I try to get my psychologist to interpret my dreams. In them, I say, I am always on my way somewhere, trying to reach some destination via the bus or the train, but am endlessly waylaid, and never arrive.

'You have a low tolerance for obstructions,' she says readily. 'You think something is going to happen to stop you getting where you're trying to go. Some obstacle.'

'Don't you think that proves I have anxiety?' I say.

She has this strategy of assuring me that I'm less anxious than I think I am; that what I'm actually afraid of is having something to be afraid of. Sometimes, however, I just want her to give me the option, to get to be anxious.

'Okay, then,' she says. In caving, she pivots smoothly over to this new reality, but her words are so wooden I can tell she views this as a capitulation. 'So everything feels difficult for you. You have a fundamental ontological anxiety. You're afraid someone is going to be able to take something away from you at any moment, and threaten your safety. You struggle to feel secure. Is that right?' She prompts. 'Eda. Yes?'

Only So Much

The shoulder bumps from strangers that make me shove back during the day go down easier at night. The power dynamic shifts when you hurry against the CBD's foot traffic as a group, newly animated with the ability to break up other clusters of bodies with your increased speed and size. On the corner of Sydney's George and Bathurst I glance up, diverted by some Big Four firm's logo beaming down – its sedate, civilised, civilising weight. The building's few lit office windows cut and blaze against the ones that have gone dark. I imagine being one of those floating Friday bodies shifting on an eighth floor, fiddling with my stationery, sipping from my mug of free pod coffee, looking out the window after dusk and realising that I should climb into my car-smelling car, return to my flat-smelling flat and kiss my cat-smelling cat. Then Ahmet falls onto his side.

'Oh, shit,' I say, coming down to my knees. I am reminded that he was the only one kind enough to help me finish off the bottle of red I'd stolen from work at the pre-drinks. 'It's a 2012 cab sav,' I'd crowed, 'it's worth like forty bucks.

Pre-mark up. We can't not finish it. Come on.' I wave my arms in tipsy semaphore to redirect foot traffic around, rather than over, his body.

'Millet, neler oluyor?' shout his friends. Cosmopolitan Turks like him who also speak English and French and leave their country of birth to hook up, drink and/or come out. From a good twenty metres ahead they half-turn their heads. Registering that our absence signifies something, they hurry back in bouncing steps, wriggling to pull down their dresses. Elif steps up and we haul Ahmet to his feet.

'Ahmet?' she says. 'Ahmetçiğim? İyi misin?' He obviously isn't – she speaks over his dry-heaves. 'We have to arrive before eleven or it's thirty dollars.'

'He needs a cab,' I say, locking eyes with Tomas, a Belgian with hair so blond and curled I suspect he's a stained-glass window baby, torn out of some European cathedral and brought to life. The son of a diplomat, he has tonight already dared a cop to fine him for jaywalking. The cop complied. Useless, but the only other man in the group in addition to Ahmet. I'm not doing the duty of taking Ahmet home because I'm not a millionaire and I don't have the energy to care for so many. And the idea of sending out a girl to care for a guy defies the unidirectionality of this sort of protective labour between friends.

'No, no, he'll be okay,' says Tomas, diplomatically. Dickhead. 'He just needs to, how you say?' He mimes sticking a finger down his throat. 'Tactical ...'

'Chunder,' I say, just as Tomas says, 'Tak-yak.' Ahmet has slumped again to the ground as we've nutted this out, eyes closing and opening like windscreen wipers set to intermittent.

Elif and the two girls from Ankara nod and commence a campaign of waking Ahmet up with gentle coaxing. In aggressive whispers, they ask him not to interrupt their evening: 'You'll feel so much better if you do it. Just try. Just give it one big try, I promise you will feel great. Kendini iyi hissedeceksin.' I feel like vomiting, it is that persuasive.

Ahmet heaves in Tomas's arms.

I mutter, 'Jesus, this is like Guantánamo, Europeans are arses,' and Tomas looks at me and says 'Really?' I had avoided wearing heels specifically for this purpose, and retreat to moral high ground. Ahmet's vomit is left where it lands beside St Andrew's Cathedral, becomes a monument to the resolve of Sydney's party people; something that will stick for a moment to the sole of a brown dress shoe as it tramps into church on Sunday morning.

*

There's glitter in my hair and down my chest but in the mirror all I see glistening is my sweat. I miss the disinterested lighting of the dance floor now – here I can observe the segment of my stomach below the belly button, which houses my organs, and protrudes no matter if I speculate that I'm dieting or eating the same but feeling worse. My face, which normally passes muster with foundation and some mascara, compared now to the complexions of the girls around me, looks as uneven as a potholed street. I try to read their smoothness like a crystal ball, but cannot tell what it portends.

I piss out the forty dollars I've spent on shots so far faster than I downed them and with more relief. The more coloured things you drink the clearer your piss is. I wonder where the colours go. Staining my insides. In India, during Holi, they catapult you with paint. I wonder at the etymology of holiday. Which came first, holy or Holi? Probably neither. I've left my purse in the cubicle. So busy was I trying to focus my eyes in the dim and grey piss-box to track the unfolding of a cubicle-wall Sharpie argument about the politics of graffiti. Blue Sharpie had argued it was a way of marking the rebellion of women against the regulation of public spaces. 'There's no female Banksy.' Black Sharpie had countered it was a slight against the working-class service staff who had to clean it up, and when I rubbed the wall experimentally found she had used permanent marker too.

I wait by the toilet door, craving a drink, reminded of the time I'd put a set of three rings, a gift from my sister Gülin (which join up to make one, somewhat like a transformer, or perhaps co-dependence), down my bra for safekeeping. Sometimes I am afraid people will rob me. Fair appraisal. I had bent down in the bathroom and the centrepiece, the silver one with the pearl in the middle, plunged into the bowl and sank to the bottom. I stared, then thought, I can't deal with this, and left. I thought, well, this is a form of robbery, and wandered back. A girl was in the cubicle by then so I knocked, as if that could prevent whatever was taking place from taking the whole damn place, and said, 'Excuse me, my ring fell into the toilet.' She flushed anyway.

I plot what to drink next as my elation wears off, and hope no one has shat on my purse. I scoot into the cubicle almost as soon as the flush goes and a redhead in Ugg boots steps out. Her cushioned soles have probably soaked up a good half-litre of piss for me. I retrieve the purse, doing my best not to touch any additional surfaces, unwilling to wash my hands a second time.

There's an electronic remix of 'Bye Bye Blackbird' playing when I emerge and make a beeline for the bar. The bass drops somewhere between verse one and the chorus, and the rhythmic pounding that follows makes me forget the original. I rifle through my wallet to the beat, wondering indistinctly if I've succeeded at tonight's sums, which I have not. I'm down an unaccounted five, which is a good twenty minutes of dead-eyed waitressing I will have to perform to recoup the loss. I can't ascertain why any thief with a face would take five dollars and not the rest of my cash, so I strike the Ugg girl off my list of suspects. I'm left with capitalism as the forerunner, as I watch it slake the thirst of a pair of men who, in identical pairs of sunnies that hide their blown pupils, chug from bottles of $6.95 San Pel in the roped-off section. Capitalism recognises the inadvisability of only stealing large sums. The hammer-and-trickle-up or some such shit.

All it means is that instead of a cocktail, I'm drinking beer. That's good. Beer calms me down. I know alcohol is a depressant, but what isn't, right? Lots of things. I mean that beer calms me down psychosomatically. It's what I drink during the day; it's what, sometimes, I drink near family. It's the missionary position of beverages.

I don't think I'd hate waiting in lines so much if it weren't for the people. Obviously. But I mean I could queue with a pack of dogs, for example. If bartenders at these sorts of places weren't so wilfully slow, didn't exercise such sweet, minimum-waged leisure in chatting to attractive patrons, I wouldn't feel as if my time had been sliced clean off my wrist and gifted to the chick sitting at the bar. I feel my soul depreciating in these moments, these ones, right now, as the guy tending the bar takes a full ten minutes, as I time it, to create a martini with a lemon twist. What's the twist? That you're a cunt? Then I dwell on the tender speed with which he penetrates each olive, as if they are all demanding care, valid and solid; then I think I'm onto something.

Once your life goal is to be an olive, it's time to abandon the whole thought process.

I stand as much like the Fearless Girl statue from Wall Street as I can – try to catch the bartender's eye with my chest out, a little bit taking the piss – but I've got no bloody chance. Instead, I'm jostled till I'm next to a gangly, laddish figure. I can only assume he's at least eighteen and merits my calling him a man, but I think it begrudgingly. He's wearing a fedora. Of course he is. He's alone, so when he opens his mouth I cave and we talk shit like:

'Hey, what's your name?'

'Oh, it's ... just pronounce it Ed-da. No, Ed ... yeah, Eva will do. Cool, where are you from?'

'I'm from the UK.'

'Sorry?'

'I'm from the UK.' He leans in for this proclamation and I lean away.

'Cool. How does the bar service here compare to there? Shit, I bet.' I'm un-Australian.

'Oh, it's fine. Already got a drink, actually; just waiting for that girl ...' he points, 'behind the bar to notice me so I can get her number.'

'Don't harass people at work, man, it's not cool. She literally can't leave or tell you off. I can promise she just wants to finish her shift and go ho –'

'But she is so hot.'

When I finish, my voice deepened by a night of reluctant shouting already, which may have made me sound more authoritative, less shrill, I'm conscious of him reappraising me as someone worth conversing with rather than manipulating into bodily contact. I'm not a yes-no on a drop-down list, the fucking nerd. So I narrow my eyes, tell him 'Nice fedora' and move further up the bar. I cannot be kind all the time. But when it comes time to order I squeeze out a please in penance when asking for a tin of anything from the club's reject-beer bin. The martini man's service is so fast it means he doesn't want to harass me sexually even a little. Such a bittersweet moment I wish 'Bye Bye Blackbird' would come back on for it.

I hoist my beer, sip it until it's too warm and the music too exhausting. It's electronic stuff I wish I knew but don't, and whose unfamiliarity comforts me not at all. And so I cave again, take my coat out of coat check and loiter on the stairs outside. By the time a third man has eye-fucked me to his fill, has asked what I'm doing, I recognise the need for a cigarette to construct for them a sense of purpose; a smokescreen, if you will.

Barely inhaling, I make sure to butt on the ground with a finger every half minute to seem like a smoker. I speculate that I could do this until I've built up around myself an ashy, salt-and-pepper crumbling cocoon or coffin. It's only because I'm an alarmist about how much longer my acquaintances can bear to be in these environments than me; and lo, one emerges. Ahmet, holding his vomit-stained full-price camel-colour Zara coat. Who gives a shit, is what I feel when I see him. In truth I do care an okay amount about him and his coat. It's a nice coat and he is a nice person. He helps me put on my hand-me-down once-was-black jacket. I help him put on his, with my fingertips.

'What are you doing out here?' I say. 'You don't smoke.'

'I'm tired,' he says, enunciating carefully, whether from the drink or the private schooling I'm not sure. 'I was thinking I will just go to my flat, actually, to finish packing.'

'Nice. I'll come with you? Do you want to hit the Macca's one last time?'

I reckon Ahmet might just be sufficiently worse for wear for me to finagle him and ... there you go, I'm right. He nods.

I won't speak to him again after he leaves. I know that only his wealth has enabled him to come to Australia on exchange, while it's only by biological happenstance that I came to be birthed out in Sydney. And that's what we in the business call a chasm.

I'm a chasm salesperson. I peddle distance. New ways to

reconceive the world such that no one is like you. I demur on speaking Turkish with Ahmet because his accent is refined, is exactly the type that my family mocks when the occasion presents. I worry I speak roughly or use outdated terminologies fed directly to me by having had only my parents to speak with, like a bird vomiting into its chicks. In my parents' beaks – mouths – I worry Turkish is a coarse inheritance. Ahmet gestures at elegant recourse to be perceived as European.

It's not, of course, particularly elegant that he has thrown up on a footpath today. I grab one of his hands to warm up in my pocket while we amble. It's a foreign city after all, Sydney. She'll make you sick.

*

During the walk across Pyrmont Bridge, Ahmet tells me about how gay men are not allowed to be conscripted into the Turkish military. It reminds me of staring at the Bosphorus, which connects Europe to Asia, with a loved one. This was back in 2012, before. Seagulls that seemed the size of albatrosses had flown alongside the ferry, circling, as she'd explained, rapt, eyes welling, how the guru she'd found in İstanbul never ate or slept. How his disciples, in their all-white uniforms, occasionally with his name in Sanskrit tattooed across their chests or down their necks, fought over who should have the honour of tying his shoes or sitting on the floor by his side on the bus to the next retreat. The Jim Jones/David Koresh–inspired con artist has been tied up in legal scandals for years now. He's gallantly defending himself by implying the women he abused liked to dress in tight clothing – to do yoga. It was a yoga cult. Sometimes I feel like cracking open my skull at the obviousness of everything.

I remember how one night I'd mentioned this ex-cult leader to Ahmet, Elif and the girls from Ankara, thinking they might have heard the story break back home. One laughed and said, 'Oh yeah, I read about him in the paper,' and made a joke.

'Sorry if I am boring you,' says Ahmet, and I snap out of it. His hand fidgets in mine. 'Which of your parents is Turkish again?'

'Oh,' I say. 'Both. My father was a major, actually. From Sivas. And my mother worked at the Population Office in the seventies and eighties in Izmir. When you were first allowed to change your gender identity. Sometimes Turkey seems so modern.'

'Oh,' he says. 'Elif said you're only half-Turkish.'

We step into the Macca's just behind three 2 am girls who stumble like it's their favoured mode of transport, holding each other and laughing, one trying to shake off her heel on the sly.

Every McDonald's reminds me of my mother. In line I think about how, when I take the train out west tomorrow, she will chide me from her sickbed for not visiting her more, for being a slut like other members of the family – which is not the right term for it – and how these sorts of things aren't about culture or time but personal integrity. I will remind myself I mustn't swipe back like I did at the boy in the fedora because the one time I did, when I said, 'Why? You got pregnant at seventeen,' she looked at me with her eyes brimming immediately with tears. 'Don't make me tell you why,' and then she told me why.

That day I had left with the intention of returning to my other life – here in the off-centre, where our existence is furnished not only with things that are essential but also with martinis with lemon twists – and had instead made it as far as the walk from the Inner West share house to Stanmore McDonald's, had sat down bathed in the fucking fluorescence and, upon opening the brown paper bag and noticing I'd been given a cheeseburger, not a chicken burger, burst into tears. It's the pickles what done it!

So you could say that I'm attached to this chain. I order and think I can make the wait for pick-up, but the crush of midnight bodies and booze lowers my blood pressure and I'm too dizzy and exhausted not to stride outside onto Darling Drive and force the crisp air in and out – quietly, so I don't seem like I'm panting. At the weight I feel I am, I'd be a sitting duck for fat jokes slid into my flesh by the tipsy hoard, like a pencil pushed down between two sweaty breasts. A chubby girl panting outside a McDonald's. It's a pickle freoccupation. Fickle preoccupation.

I step out after the girls, watching as they sustain themselves against the wind buffeting their hair into their sticky, glossy lips, resilient despite the hours. Ahmet waits patiently inside, because he is patient. I slide to the asphalt although I'm wearing a dress. I am a poor dresser in that I usually wear clothes for chairs and so sit on chairs.

A man approaches me. When I look back on it I'll remember only that he had stubble and wore something yellow. Perhaps a large footpath French fry. I stand quickly before he can crouch.

'What are you doing down there?' he says. Summoning the preoccupation men have with female loitering, the perceived strangeness of actions that aren't really that strange. My responding 'Just waiting for someone' isn't broad enough, I suppose, from a life of flattening my accent, rounding my Rs instead of letting them peter out, for comprehensibility to migrants, and so he next asks, 'Where are you from?'

I say, 'Here, but my parents are, you know, ethnic, I assume that's what you want ... mean.'

He takes up the ethnic custom of kissing me on both my cheeks. I let it slide. He asks my name and I say, 'Yeah, Ada is fine', and he takes this information as being just as precious except his kisses devolve closer to my mouth, one almost snaring me. I know this game. Not a good sport, but I've played it. I wonder if he really considers that I might fall disoriented onto his flaccid, moist tongue. I want to say something like 'I don't fuck rapists' but it's needlessly inflammatory for when I repeat this story later. People will jibber jabber about my being harsh and forego sympathy, so I look around furiously until Ahmet appears. As he steps up the other man steps away, then recedes, I suppose surmising that I've already been claimed, like a seat on a bus.

I don't mean to snatch the brown bag Ahmet holds out but I do. My hand is shaking so he takes it and puts it in his pocket. I roll my eyes, sick in my bones in these moments, these ones, right now, of men, and retract my hand. I slide down onto the stoop of a closed boutique store paying four grand a month in rent and carrying about four pieces of clothing inside. Ahmet sits down next to me.

'I'm just hungry,' I say. I press the fries into my mouth horizontally so more will go in at once. 'Fuck, you wouldn't believe what happened while you were inside.'

'Hmm?' he says, slanting his gaze sideways. I'm relieved I don't have to worry about him trying to kiss me. A nice person with a nice coat, whom my mother wants me to marry but with whom I can barely share a Happy Meal.

I tell him about the other guy and he says, 'Eek, why didn't you kick him?'

I open the box in my lap, notice it's a cheeseburger and not a chicken burger. I wish I had a reaction to offer Ahmet but am plain out. I feel about as bland and plastic as the cheeseburger I will eat anyway. This shit's in my veins, or my arteries, like it isn't in Ahmet's. As he nibbles away beside me I think about how when I was seven years old my father took me to Macca's every afternoon for two months, knocking off his worksite around six and beyond cooking, till I got big and round like my favourite McDonald's mascot, Grimace. 'I did not know any better,' my father told me later, 'I didn't know, bilmiyordum.' I think about how in Turkey they eat tripe soup (işkembe çorbası) after they've had a night out. That word, işkembe, always takes me a moment to recall, because it sounds to my second-gen ears too much like another word – işkence, torture. It's at that point in the evening when every additional interaction feels like işkence, like it would take an epi-pen to the thigh to muster up the energy to form a complete sentence. But I can't tell Ahmet this, can't tell him much of anything.

All I can think to say to Ahmet is, 'How would you feel if you saw a girl who looks like she's just chatting really friendly to a man against a brick wall, then go from zero to a hundred and strike his dick?' But I fear our English levels, or something else, have not converged on this point. We finish our meals and then our friendship. I go home and he goes home. Darling Harbour stays where it landed, not really a midpoint between Blacktown and the Bosphorus.

Gothic Body, in Two Parts

Part 1
Anthropophagy

My mother has always dieted as if trying to practise necromancy.

Last month, she walked me through her newest diet regimen. She eats exactly seven grapes, and one fig, which she has cut up into small segments, to ensure she ingests the right combination of chemicals. I watch her carefully pry apart a sticky dried fig in her hands, portioning methodically. She eats one grape, then one seventh of a fig, fearfully and wondrously. Then another grape and another seventh of a fig. This, she says, is the ultimate fat loss method.

As a child Gülin would drive her to her SureSlim appointments every second weekend. At the office, my mother's weight loss coach would be waiting, a folder clasped to his chest, ready to hand over my mother's latest diet plan, something obeyed as if it had been inscribed upon a stone tablet and passed down a mountain. One boiled egg and three olives for breakfast. A lettuce wrap for lunch, made using only wholesome Mountain Bread, which was the most joyless bread you could find before gluten-free became widely available. Every Saturday on our weekly trips to Westpoint shopping centre, my sister and I would down our McDonald's or KFC and my mother would peel her egg and eat it.

We grew fat while she grew no thinner. Some days I'd return home from school to find her wearing a garbage bag like an ersatz pair of pants she had punctured holes in, cycling on the second-hand stationary bicycle my father bought her, trying to sweat the fat off her body. Other days, when my sister was a teen and I a tween, she took us to the pharmacy to buy my sister diet pills for her sudden weight gain.

I struggle to differentiate her behaviour from prayer, from the way I worry at my fingernails, ingesting the hangnails, or the way I carefully appliquéd the word 'FAT' to my stomach with texta when I was twelve. I struggle to differentiate us, we who have inherited this gaze, these eyes which cannot see ourselves kindly and cannot see each other kindly.

I try to understand her overfeeding of us, even of my big fat dog.

Television tells me she is a whimsical ethnic mother, trying to plug a hole in us through our mouths, looking for a shortcut to satisfy us, fulfil us, find a way of knowing that our life is improved by her hand in real time. You think, 'Oh, this is just an ethnic stereotype – the Italian nonna who wants to feed her babies, the Greek or Mediterannean or Middle

Eastern lady in the apron who won't let you leave her house before you take home a Tupperware container loaded up with leftovers or eat a bowl of goodbye fruit.'

There's a less rotund edge to this whole performance. The overly large portions that could feed two or three. If I, to this day, don't finish these plates, a sort of dance begins, wherein my mother or my sister loom over me, circle me, chidingly, mockingly, asking, over and over, 'Why aren't you eating? I bet you're dieting again, huh? You're not even that fat. You just need to lose some weight from your hips.' My mother.

'Wow, oh my God, you're soooo skinny, you're just like soooo healthy.' Dilek.

I may as well not be there, I try to tell myself – they are merely playing out some gross pantomime under lights so bright I appear only in silhouette. Audience participation is not required.

'No,' I say, nonetheless, weakly.

Never use the words 'I'm full' or the vultures will start to cluster, crowd around, assemble, and needle you until you're empty inside again, doing things to make sure you suddenly fancy the idea of eating until you feel pain, a tiny act of self-harm. They insist you eat a slice of cake for dessert or load up your plate and watch you till you're so stressed and sad that you do take a bite because – it's easier. It's easier to move towards disorder.

I announced my first diet at age nine, before I knew fully what I meant. It was as if I was repeating a word learned by ear, via immersion, because your society does not only teach you how to speak but also what to say.

My psychologist theorises once that perhaps my mother is trying to insulate us, equip us with a fine layer of blubber which might deter our rapists-in-waiting. That old joke we used to say as kids, about fat people being harder to kidnap.

I demur, agree for a second, and come close to believing that this desire of hers to protect us also runs alongside her wish to police our bodies. It reminds me about a holiday we took together in Newcastle five years ago. I remember we walked along Nobbys Head toward the lighthouse, slowly, hitting upon a tall patch of grass where it was suddenly just me and my mother and a man. She stopped mid-sentence, said, 'Eda, I'm scared,' and I hurried us away, while the man barely looked up from his fishing rod and line.

To this psychologist I one day find myself caught in a loop, can't stop repeating the same sentence – and I'm thankful she gets paid as well as she does, to listen to this shit that seems deep to me, but isn't, as I repeat, over and over – 'I'm her mother,' I say. 'I'm her mother. I'm her mother.' I'm not.

That theory doesn't quite hold water to me, though. I can't help but ask why this selfsame mother criticises me and my sister for our weights, likes to point out how her legs are thin while ours are not. How my formless clothes make me look as if I have shit my pants. How our partners won't want to fuck us if we keep blowing up like inflatable pool toys.

When I gained a sudden and inexplicable amount of weight in 2015, ten kilos in a year, then twenty-five in three, which came upon me as if overnight, no one thought to ask whether something was wrong – which, of course, it was.

Instead, my mother pounced upon it as an opportunity to ensure that I start to dress more conservatively.

'Barış called you a slut the other day,' she said to me. 'I wanted to disagree but he saw the way you dress. You can't dress like that anymore.'

She smiled smugly like the face she would pull while we ate our KFC and she ate her single boiled, slimy SureSlim egg.

*

My first memory is of my first nightmare. When I was four I woke up in bed, crying, replaying the dream I had just had: that all the children in my preschool class had made sandwiches out of themselves, placed two giant slices of bread on either side of their body and gone to town. It has caused something of a fascination with self-cannibalisation. I think often about how the human body, when it goes hungry, starts to digest itself, stomach acid chewing into stomach lining.

It's what makes this one line of a story I read about ten years ago so memorable, a story I encountered at the height of my interest in anonymous chat forums and the internet phenomenon of 'creepy pasta'. One of the most famous creepy-pasta people wrote under the name Josef K, and to this day I couldn't tell you anything about anything he's ever written, except these two things: that his best story, the favourite of his fans, is entitled 'Sick, or The Algorithm'. It's about a man who lives in a town where an omniscient presence off-screen has poisoned all his food, but only his. He throws up everything he eats, every day, because the poisoner is one step ahead at all times, has corrupted everything he tries to eat, even things he steals, even the food in houses he picks at random the next town over. Finally, in desperation, he breaks into one final house, and instead of eating the food he finds, this man performs the truly unexpected: he kills and eats the occupant.

Julia Kristeva, in 'Powers of Horror: An Essay on Abjection', explains what makes it, sometimes, so horrific to have a body, what makes it a source of horror and disgust. Under the heading 'The Improper/Unclean', she writes about

> loathing an item of food, a piece of filth, waste, or dung. The spasms and vomiting that protect me. The repugnance, the retching that thrusts me to the side and turns me away from defilement, sewage, and muck. The shame of compromise, of being in the middle of treachery. The fascinated start that leads me toward and separates me from them. Food loathing is perhaps the most elementary and most archaic form of abjection. When the eyes see or the lips touch that skin on the surface of milk – harmless, thin as a sheet of cigarette paper, pitiful as a nail paring – I experience a gagging sensation and, still farther down, spasms in the stomach, the belly; and all the organs shrivel up the body, provoke tears and bile, increase heartbeat, cause forehead and hands to perspire ... But since the food is not an 'other' for 'me,' who am only in their desire, I expel myself, I spit myself out, I abject myself within the same motion through which 'I'

claim to establish myself ... During that course in which 'I' become, I give birth to myself amid the violence of sobs, of vomit. Mute protest of the symptom, shattering violence of a convulsion that, to be sure, is inscribed in a symbolic system, but in which, without either wanting or being able to become integrated in order to answer to it, it reacts, it abreacts. It abjects.

The second and last thing I remember is the quote. It appears in another story I was sure Josef K wrote, but which I have since checked with him and discovered he did not, although it alters little about the memory I carried with me for so many years. In this other unattributed story, now lost to the abyss of anonymous imageboards, about two or three friends are boarded up in the upper storey of a house, waiting for zombies or beasts or evil wizards to finally break in and kill and eat them. One of the characters turns to the other and muses out loud, 'God. Of everything we've lost, what have we gained?'

Part 2
Fuck You David,
And Your Little David Too

It's perhaps not surprising that I viscerally reacted against femininity when I was young. Throughout puberty I wore two bras – three bras, sometimes – in an attempt to stop having tits. I put little white stickers over my areolas so I would feel less like I had tits, without experiencing body dysmorphia per se. I only wanted to be smooth, not visible from the outside. And I would think gory things about wanting to slice them clean off. It was all shame. I felt ashamed about having these body parts which felt like targets on my back. Like I'd accidentally handed someone a list of my most embarrassing moments and greatest fears.

Weight marks us in a similar way – tells others that we're supposedly imperfect, how we're imperfect, and that there's an easy inroad into criticising and oppressing us. Concerned trolls will use it to cannily deduce that there's something wrong in our personal lives, on the level of our unconscious, or that we aren't entirely self-actualised, or are lazy, or perhaps have poor time management. Frat boys on the street will use it to call you a tub of lard or a whale and high-five their friends. Two sides of the same coin.

There are countless other ways in which our bodies tell on us, provide others with these inroads. Having a body deemed unlivable or uninhabitable, which nevertheless we do inhabit, makes it so that anyone who is seeking a way to make you feel bad, to assert their power over you, doesn't need to look very hard – only at the colours of our skin, the ways we walk, talk. Our bodies give themselves away, as plain as the noses on our faces. Or the people we go home with, or send texts to, or long for after midnight. Being embodied is to seem to overshare in every moment.

Judith Butler, in her book *Bodies That Matter: On The Discursive Limits of Sex,* writes that bodies, for all their materiality, are also made in the social world, by gaining their meaning in the social world. Of course a body is something one can reach out and touch, feel, but it is also a canvas upon which different meanings are projected. These meanings supply a script that, in turn, produces our own behaviour: we learn, as we grow, what it means to be a woman, rather than it coming to us inherently. We then act on this unconscious knowledge, conforming our bodies to what it means to be a woman, through hair, dress or making our selves small, for example. Butler writes that, 'if certain constructions appear constitutive, that is, have this character of being that "without which" we could not think at all, we might suggest that bodies only appear, only endure, only live within the productive constraints of certain highly gendered regulatory schemas.' The disciplinary quality of gender as constitutive radically limits our range of options for what we can acceptably be, and those who do not adhere to gendered regulatory schemas are punished. Butler goes on:

> Given this understanding of construction as constitutive
> constraint, is it still possible to raise the critical question
> of how such constraints not only produce the domain
> of intelligible bodies, but produce as well a domain of
> unthinkable, abject, unlivable bodies? This latter domain
> is not the opposite of the former, for oppositions are,
> after all, part of intelligibility; the latter is the excluded
> and illegible domain that haunts the former domain
> as the spectre of its own impossibility, the very limit to
> intelligibility, its constitutive outside.

Once, while riding a nightrider after an evening out with Justin, I noticed a young, white, sloppy-drunk-seeming guy observing us with surprisingly clear eyes – while his head bobbed, his bloodshot eyes didn't stray. We had taken a seat almost in the back of the bus, a zone two massive nerds like us would normally avoid, ingrained from childhood, but I was fatigued from the six to eight drinks I had imbibed and less hypervigilant about my safety than I might otherwise have been were I more sober, or older like I am now. I had my eyes closed, head on Justin's shoulder. He had removed my glasses to make me more comfortable, and placed them in the deep pocket of his button-down flannel.

This guy sitting in the seat in front, who tracked us as we got on, eventually spun around in his seat, detecting an unprotected woman, and after watching me for a while leant over to my partner and remarked, 'Hey man, your bitch is really out of it.'

As if impressed. The white guy was busy eyeballing Justin, who for his part wasn't engaging, had his eyes fixed nervously frontward, and so they both missed my snap back to attention.

Butler continues:

And further, this imperative, this injunction, requires
and institutes a "constitutive outside" – the unspeakable,
the unviable, the nonnarrativizable that secures and,
hence, fails to secure the very borders of materiality.
The normative force of performativity – its power to
establish what qualifies as "being" – works not only

through reiteration, but through exclusion as well.
And in the case of bodies, those exclusions haunt
signification as its abject borders or as that which is
strictly foreclosed: the unlivable, the nonnarrativizable,
the traumatic.

'Nice glasses,' the white guy said to my partner, after another moment of keen assessment, searching for a way in. A shot across the bow – he had found a chink in our armour. A pathway into power, a visual landing strip, access to a shortcut sure-fire method of making us feel small. All bullies say the same things and know to say the same things. They draw upon established power relations which exist as a resource, which flow through the general populace and can be called upon like the Force at any given moment. It's fucking Foucauldian.

Four eyes, this guy was saying, just like I got told when I was six and seven and eight and nine at public school.

In his lectures published under the title *Society Must be Defended*, Michel Foucault says,

> Do not regard power as a phenomenon of mass and
> homogeneous domination – the domination of one
> individual over others, of one group over others, or
> of one class over others … Power is exercised through
> networks, and individuals do not simply circulate in
> those networks; they are in a position to both submit
> to and exercise this power. They are never the inert or
> consenting targets of power; they are always its relays …

The individual is not, in other words, power's opposite number; the individual is one of power's first effects. The individual is in fact a power effect, and at the same time, and to the extent that he is a power-effect, the individual is a relay: power passes through the individuals it has constituted.

My partner remained silent. I quickly retrieved my glasses and propped them back on my nose, a drunken gesture of defiance or solidarity. No pasarán sort of shit. The white guy pivoted his head back to look at me. Noticed the glasses that had appeared on my nose seemingly out of nowhere.

'Oh,' he said, rearing back, and falling quiet. We lost his interest.

I seethed and seethed, and for the entire bus ride eavesdropped on the vile conversation he was having with his friend. My concentration became singular. I took careful notes – I had to. The way to insult him wasn't written on his face like my gender was or our glasses were. All I managed to ascertain is that his name was David. This felt like enough. You can do a lot with David. When we stood up to get off at our stop, his attention turned back to us like I expected it would, and he tried to throw one last lob.

His grand pronouncement, as my partner moved to walk past him down the aisle:

'Hey,' said David. 'Hey. Hey. You're Asian.'

That was it – it was easy. Inside the Australian public consciousness lies racism, thrumming sub-surface, and it is drawn upon whenever it becomes necessary to make someone else feel bad, usually on public transport. Fatness is a joke; non-whiteness is a joke; femaleness is a joke; presenting as queer or trans or non-binary, all jokes. It's easy. You might even do it, without wanting to. When you find yourself getting mad at, say, a person of colour who takes too long asking the bus driver a question. You get agitated – it happens. You just want to go home. You think, but would never say, 'Oh my God, can you just go back to where you came from?'

It's easy, because you've been taught not just how to speak, but also what to say.

Before my partner had a chance to jump in – not that he would have, he was as non-confrontational then as I am at present, now that I have developed a deeper regard for my safety – I issued the line I had prepared, to David.

It was all I could think to say: 'And you're a cunt, David. You're a stupid cunt.'

In her book *The Gothic Body: Sexuality, Materialism, and Degeneration at the Fin de Siécle,* Kelly Hurley writes about the abhuman:

> In place of a human body stable and integral (at
> least, liable to no worse than the ravages of time and
> disease), fin-de-siecle Gothic offers the spectacle of a
> body metamorphic and undifferentiated; in place of
> the possibility of human transcendence, the prospect
> of an existence circumscribed within the realities of
> gross corporeality; in place of a unitary and securely
> bounded human subjectivity, one that is both

fragmented and permeable. Within this genre one may witness the relentless destruction of 'the human' and the unfolding in its stead of what I will call, to borrow an evocative term from supernaturalist author William Hope Hodgson, the 'abhuman'. The abhuman subject is a not-quite-human subject, characterized by its morphic variability, continually in danger of becoming not-itself, becoming other. The prefix 'ab-' signals a movement away from a site or condition, and thus a loss. But a movement away from is also a movement towards –towards a site or condition as yet unspecified – and thus entails both a threat and a promise ... The Fin-de-siecle Gothic is positioned within precisely such an ambivalence: convulsed by nostalgia for the 'fully human' subject whose undoing it accomplishes so resolutely, and yet aroused by the prospect of a monstrous becoming. One may read its obsessive staging and restaging of the spectacle of abhumanness as a paralysis, a species of trauma, but one must also note the variety and sheer exuberance of the spectacle, as the human body collapses and is reshapen across an astonishing range of morphic possibilities: into slug-men, snake-women, ape-men, beast-people, octopus-seal-men, beetle-women, dog-men, fungus-people.

As we legged it out of the bus, I overheard his friend lean down and say, distantly, but in shock, 'How did she know your name?', as if convinced I had performed witchcraft. I hadn't even insulted him; all I could do was invoke his name in an attempt to reclaim some power, some information, some way in which he told on himself in the ways that marginalised bodies tell on themselves all the time. The best part about the whole thing was a guy who had been sitting at the front of the bus the whole time, uninvolved, and who got out at the same stop a mere moment after us, called out at my back, right before we took off in opposite directions: 'What did you say?'

And I said, 'Not you, mate, I wasn't talking to you.'

And he said, 'Oh, weird. My name is also David.'

And I thought to myself, trudging home in the dark, occasionally catching a glimpse of a bat hanging, asleep, from a tree, as I reflected on that final encounter, *Wow, isn't that uncanny.*

Shit-eating

I see us eating well without living well. Most people in my social circle readily identify as 'foodies', having grown up consuming a steady diet of *MasterChef* and aesthetically busted avocado on toast. At a friend's most recent birthday party, we twenty-somethings gathered in a circle to feast on 'nduja and organic honey; we scooped up the latter with tiny spoons after gently cracking through the raw honeycomb's wooden frame, which oozed and spilled out in pornographic slow motion. None of us will ever own a home. My friend's flat was a nearly condemned building in Chippendale with black mould climbing up the walls, rented out primarily to students precisely because of their low standards and its proximity to Sydney University. The following week, the kitchen shelves fell from the wall in one piece, shattering all their glassware into all their food.

When I indulge in something cutting edge with brioche or fennel or goat's cheese or edible flowers, it's most often eaten at home. But I'm not wrapped in a dressing gown, with freshly moisturised legs, splayed across my chaise lounge. Instead, I'm in my pyjamas, bra-less and with my skin broken out, because I am too tired to have cooked anything. What these moments usually mean is that I have finished my 'work-done-at-work', and now upon arriving home have to complete the work that is supposed to be more leisurely because it's 'work-done-at-home'.

When I was fifteen, I watched episodes of *MasterChef* sitting in front of a bowl of home brand mac 'n' cheese I had microwaved myself for dinner. Call me aspirational. It's easy, I think, and tempting, to congratulate the increased accessibility of being able to self-identify as a foodie – after all, the existence of things like degustations at different price points make a formerly bourgeois experience accessible to youths and the middle class. We could interpret this as a sign of upward mobility into a class we may, in fact, never succeed at entering. But it's also one that we probably should not aspire to enter.

Another term for this argument is the 'Charcuterie Discourse', so-called (by me) following a recent protracted Twitter argument between different factions of the left regarding whether charcuterie is bourgeois and anti-communist, and whether we all should or should not get to eat it. The negative argument is as follows: rich people can afford to eat it and you don't want to be rich, do you? That's a shootable offence. The affirmative argument tries a different tack: taste is not classed, smoked meats are delightful regardless of who you are, and we should all want them for our comrades. If everyone got to be middle class and enjoy middle class–coded treats, then that would mean there was no such thing as class because we would all be able to access luxury. To that I will say: charcuterie is, in fact, Islamophobic. Think about it. And then invest in my halal charcuterie start-up.

I think about this particular instantiation of foodie culture as an Australian export, dispersed via the soft power of *MasterChef* Australia. Have you ever watched any other *MasterChef* series? They prepare sandwiches. They prepare eggs. Eggs made of eggs, and not a nine-component dessert crafted to look like an egg. Not the simulacrum of an egg, but an actual egg. How embarrassing.

There is no more ham-heavy, charcuterie-oriented land than Spain, where I lived for six months in 2014. And yet, Spanish people my age thought the notion of queuing to eat some place special rather offensive – they usually preferred to go to the tapería closest to their flat, with the cheapest tinto, where they would smoke and share unremarkable tortilla de patatas and montaditos on white bread. During my time in Spain, I stopped drinking coffee wholesale, unable to stomach the torrefacto beans. There was also the question of the coffee-making itself: staff would turn on the milk wand on a several-thousand-euro espresso machine, letting it sputter, positively shouting and spewing into the jug in agony, while they walked away, pottered, and laconically returned much later; what you got after this inexpert ordeal was burnt shit.

In Australia, gourmet culture manifests in a strange winner-takes-all: one place will have a queue wrapped down the street, while its next-door neighbour will quietly go under. When I was twenty-one, I worked at a cafe on King Street in Sydney's Newtown called Zamba Flavours, which was run by an Argentinian family. Four weeks after opening, they suddenly stopped giving me shifts; I had two other jobs so I never followed up, figuring they were experiencing teething pains. Two weeks later, the cafe's doors were shuttered, replaced by a Lentil As Anything.

Learning to make coffee as a barista in Australia, we were directed to never let the wand produce any sound other than that of paper tearing: crisp, clean, quiet and intentional. This was supposed to introduce the smallest possible bubbles of air into the milk and help to generate a foam that looked like wet paint, rather than dish soap. Australia has a coffee culture, I would try to explain to European friends my age: it was a point of pride that we had single-handedly managed to drive Starbucks out of the continent. They thought largely that I was a snob, I think, and obnoxious, until the day I heard from another Australian that an Australian cafe – as it was described on its website, and now a widespread phenomenon across Europe – was operating in Malasaña, the Newtown of Madrid. There I had my first cup of Spanish coffee that didn't make me want to kill myself. Which was funny, because I always want to kill myself, in a way that has no relation to whether I do or do not have access to brunch.

All of this is not to say that other cultures in other countries don't enjoy brunch. But I do think they don't do brunch the way Australians do it. Here's how I would describe it if I were a semiotician, you were uninitiated and this was an important topic.

What is commonly dubbed 'doing brunch' – rather than 'having brunch' – involves visiting a cafe some time before two in the afternoon on a weekend. These cafes are typically located on the main streets in the suburbs of Sydney's Inner West, Melbourne's Inner North, or in the alleyways of Adelaide and Hobart CBDs. At brunch, customers order a combination of food and drinks chosen from a menu.

Drinks typically include coffee – namely cold brew or espresso, with or without frothed milk; loose leaf rather than bagged tea; blended ice drinks; fresh or 'cold-pressed' juice and smoothies, offering a variety of combinations of fruit, vegetable, seed or other 'health food' and 'superfood' ingredients. Meals include quintessential breakfast fare, usually featuring a selection of several types of bread (most notably sourdough), combined with egg (customers are given the option of choosing how their egg is prepared: either poached, fried or scrambled), and a 'protein' (typically smoked salmon, ham, bacon, poached chicken, haloumi or mushroom).

Of course, there are many other permutations available to the brunch customer, but I have briefly surveyed the conventional location, drink and meal options. This is in order to make a broader point, not just about variety, but also choice. A core component of brunch is that the customer is empowered to choose how they consume. Would they like to sit inside or outside? What type of bread? How would you like your eggs prepared? How would you like your coffee: cold brew, three quarters full, extra hot, double shot, decaf? Menus list food offerings not as a metonym for all the ingredients a dish contains, like 'cheeseburger'. Instead, they list out each ingredient, optimising the control the customer has over their consumption. If a name is given to the menu item, the emphasis is on humour, such as a pun like 'Eggscellent Delight', rather than on symbolic efficiency. This breakdown in signification suggests that brunch is filled with new meanings beyond the literal, and which evacuate the possibility of viewing it as a source of 'unhealthy', 'unpleasant', 'generic' or 'fast' food.

In addition to being endlessly customisable according to the whims of each customer, brunch is also bountiful. Food is plated in such a way as to emphasise quantity – either in intentionally over-large servings, as share-plates, or on platters which maximise the food's surface area. This emphasis on bounty is exhibited by the recent addition of the 'bottomless' beverage – bottomless sparkling water, bottomless mimosas, bottomless sangrias. It is rather interesting that the phrase 'bottomless beverage' dominates, rather than a pre-existing phrase which captures the same idea: 'free refills'. I argue that the latter term is more readily connected to the experience of having fast food.

On a basic level, both fast food and brunch are similar experiences. Both entail eating food that one has purchased. On an ideological level, however, brunch emerges as the antithesis of fast food. I say this for the following four reasons.

First, brunch is slow: customers are able to take their time, choose exactly what they would like, and, after the dining experience, spend added hours at the cafe – whether this means drinking, chatting, reading a book or working on their laptop.

Second, one does not serve themselves brunch. At a fast food restaurant, the customer has to wait in line to order, choosing from a menu so fixed that one could eat the same meal at any one of hundreds of other restaurants across the globe; if they want another drink, they must stand up and refill it themselves. By contrast, table service at brunch is most common and encouraged. The customer is waited on and has their refuse cleaned up on their behalf by waitstaff. In addition, chain restaurants are rarely part of the brunch experience[1] as customers place a high premium on one-of-a-kind experiences: local venues serving local ingredients.

Third, while the meaning associated with fast food is that it is unhealthy, brunch is viewed as a nutritional and nourishing meal.

Finally, fast food is conceptualised as being for the poor – blue-collar workers, single parents, broke students. By contrast, being able to afford brunch suggests the comfort of your class status. This functions in two ways: first, if you can afford to pay the financial cost (which is accepted as being high almost to the point of it being a joke, if one looks at the

---

1   Chain restaurants rarely survive Australian cafe culture. See the mass
     closures of Starbucks and Gloria Jean's, for example.

discourse surrounding the 'smashed avo'), and second, if you can afford to while away hours on a weekend.

Another facet of brunch is that it is visually stunning. Emphasis is placed on the aesthetic value of the food and drinks. For example, lattes with the more complex art (say, a swan rather than a floret) are more highly prized, despite this feature not altering the taste of the beverage. Attention is paid to plating, and ingredients whose value stems either from their novelty or appearance are used, such as edible flowers, brightly coloured berries and spices like turmeric.[2] This visual appeal and emphasis of brunch means that it is the most frequently photographed meal – pictures of plates are regularly shared on social media, suggesting that the experience of brunch enjoys a second life in the digital realm as a source of social capital. There is a whole industry of influencers whose job it is to spruik the art of brunch, ranking individual cafes. Indeed, the highest searched phrase which follows the coinage 'Instagrammable' – that is, worthy of photographing and placing on Instagram – according to Google auto-complete, is 'Instagrammable cafes near me'.

Brunch's connection to choice, plenitude and health suggest that late-capitalist society values brunch as a luxury or leisure activity. Therefore, the concept of brunch plays a vital role in reproducing class due to its associations with

---

2   Turmeric lattes have been popular for a few years in the brunch scene. Of course, turmeric blended with milk has been a traditional (and, before their popularisation in the west, viewed negatively as an inexpensive and unsophisticated) 'home remedy' among non-white cultures for some time.

bourgeois lifestyle and taste, an argument that is only reinforced when one considers brunch's associations with time and money. Brunch's typical placement on a weekend also explicates who it is intended 'for' – individuals who do not engage in work on a weekend are most often members of the white-collar and affluent classes, served by waitstaff who are required to work on the weekends. The use of brunch to paint an image of one's lifestyle suggests it is a conspicuous consumption activity, rather than one used to generate sociality or community. As with other acts of conspicuous leisure, such as long games of cricket played by the English upper classes on a Sunday, these factors suggest that brunch is used to maintain and reproduce the leisure classes.

End of thought experiment.

I think most of what I've written is correct, from the point of view of ideology. I've written it as if I were an academic, because that's what I'm trying to be. But here's the negative argument now. Although brunch is a bourgeois cultural activity, I and others like me who might partake in it – young creative and knowledge workers – are not bourgeois. We are role-playing to cover up for the fact that we not bourgeois. In her 2019 book *Capital is Dead: Is This Something Worse?*, McKenzie Wark writes of information, or knowledge, workers, like me:

> The hacker class experiences extremes of a winner-take-all outcome of its efforts. On the one hand, fantastic careers and the spoils of some simulation of the old bourgeois lifestyle; on the other hand, precarious and

part-time work, start-ups that go bust, and the making
routine of our jobs by new algorithms – designed
by others of our very own class. The hacker class
was supposed to be a privileged one, shielded from
proletarianization by its creativity and technical skill.
But it too can be made casual and precarious.

I don't know about you, but what I do with all the time
I save, or serotonin I generate, is either experience my leisure
time in the form of a commodity, or use it to work and
produce commodities. When I worked at Zamba Flavours, I
was an exploited casual, just as I was at all the other cafes that
made me wear silly uniforms, and who gave me no breaks
and paid me no super. And I continue to be an exploited
casual now, even though I no longer work in hospitality. I
can't remember the last time I didn't work on a weekend;
didn't feel surveilled at work; didn't not own the fruits of
my labour; didn't feel so precarious it made me mentally ill,
stumbling between contracts and unable to predict what my
income or job will be three or six months from now.

No dining experience can make up for any of this. There
is not a single pop-up, rooftop, themed and/or alleyway
bar on earth that could make an outing so satisfying that
it erases from memory every other moment of indignity.
Still, for some of us, eating something not-shit has become
such an unwavering desire that it risks rising to the level of
pathology. Have you ever watched a friend, or been that
friend, who scrolls online dining listings with urgency,
unable to bring themselves to eat anywhere that does not

have a four-point-something rating based on at least ten reviews? Are you okay? I'm not. Carbonated wine doesn't cure my depression; table service or customisable burgers at McDonald's don't cure my depression; and superfoods certainly don't cure my depression, but they probably, at least a little, make me more depressed in their failure to make me less depressed.

Don't get me wrong. My disposable income is higher than it was, and my earnings place me in the top 20 per cent in the world; I don't need to shoplift brie anymore, I can just put it straight into my basket. I stand here as a beneficiary of neoliberalism, on the receiving end, sometimes, of an UberEats delivery from a gig worker who hates me, or a meal served on a board rather than a plate by a bored waiter who makes no penalty rates. And this economy hinges on the marketing campaigns that advertise both of us, to each other, as being perfectly content, as well as requiring that we never speak to each other and compare notes, and discover, in fact, that we are not. We are not content and we are unable to tolerate this anymore, and if we knew this about each other, or acknowledged it in ourselves, we might rise up, as a result, in union, and organise as a collective, as if our liberation, not just our misery, was interdependent. I, on my side of the labour relation, am an exemplar of hustle culture. I rise, I grind, I do what I love. I 'eat a coffee for lunch', and sleep is for the weak, and my eye bags have eye bags, and this cute new app I found reminds me to drink water and to water my plants, which are dead, and my colleague loaned me two Valiums, to deploy at strategic moments, only when

I can't sit in the office for an eleventh hour, marking essays, for even one second longer, because they give me panic attacks, and now that my insides are numb thanks to the Valium, I can't eat out and I can't get eaten out.

My friend Cher Tan, a writer who has dealt with a plethora of shit jobs, including neoliberal food delivery services, conjures up the other side of this labour relation, via an image of the joyfully empowered gig economy worker: 'In these companies' promotional material aimed at recruiting "partners", the ability to "be your own boss" is often invoked.' I imagine some possibly coked up private sector consultant writing in a 2019 strategy paper for Uber Australia, 'Uber provides opportunities for more than 60 000 driver-partners in Australia who value the flexibility it offers. Many driver-partners couldn't work without the flexibility Uber offers. Uber provides economic opportunities for more than 60 000 driver-partners in Australia. Using the Uber app enables these workers to earn income when and where they want, fitting their work in with their preferences and commitments. The type of flexibility Uber offers driver-partners is rare.'

One must imagine the food delivery partner happy: he loves it, this is the best job he's ever had; he's just driving part-time to pay off student loans before he launches his start-up; he's not on the edge of being deported because his asylum application was rejected; he's just doing this for some pocket change, a bit of extra cash for shows on the weekend. Gigs for gigs: for shits and giggles.

But I'm not laughing. If I'm smiling, it's only because I'm glad that the meal comes in a paper bag, because that's one less thing in the house to contemplate asphyxiating myself with. You say I joke about suicide, but at least I can admit how unhappy I am. I'm unhappy. We have that in common. Let's hold that in common. I'm not having a good time; neither of us are.

Kalıtsal

There's a folk legend on my father's side of the family, passed down by word-of-mouth, that we are distantly descended from members of the Qajar dynasty, which ruled over Iran until 1925. The words 'Kacar Hasan' appear on a family tree my mother created on my sister's behalf, a grade-seven school assignment that would have been easy to complete for those other children whose lineage was rich enough to document. I mean rich literally: permanent patronymic surnames and other population-documenting measures like the taking of the census are recent inventions designed to systematise drawing taxes out of the population, and to regulate private property. Historically, therefore, those who have maintained a carefully pruned and legible family tree – royalty and powerful families who can point back hundreds of years to their forebears – have only done so because they stood to gain something from the knowledge: an inheritance.

My mother has approximated parts of this tree and curated it in others, hanging onto it intentional errata like baubles. My eldest sister's legal surname is not listed, and my father's surname appears instead; my parents' year of marriage is omitted, replaced with a date the year before my eldest sister's birth. As a consequence, my father's age is listed as four years older than he is, and my father's third brother doesn't appear at all, making it appear as if he has only three siblings. Per this piece of paper, my parents married each other at age eighteen and nineteen respectively. A ridiculous domino effect of lies designed to hide the originary incident, for which my family bears no blame. I think about my mother thinking through all this bullshit, re-crafting a version of events for herself, carefully shifting textboxes on Microsoft Paint, eighteen years ago. In Turkey, before she migrated, she worked for many years in Births, Deaths and Marriages as a census officer, one of the few women in this role, helping to make the contours of the population of the young Republic knowable to the state. Rural children, in particular those from villages, were often presented to her in groups of two or three, with families generally not making the trip into the city to have them registered until they were done having children. She explains that some glib parent would often, in answer to her question, 'What is his age?', simply remark, 'Why don't you guess?', and thrust their three- or four-year-old before her. My mother has made up many dates.

I have the only copy of the tree that exists. It is a crude diagram, taking up one A4 piece of paper, put together in Microsoft Paint using a series of pink and blue textboxes and uni-directional arrows. A few years ago, I dug it up out of a box like treasure and kept it. Hasan is my father's most distant known ancestor, and is reported to have fled Iran with his

brother Hüseyin and arrived in Turkey in 1870, to the village
of Çentik, near Sivas. By way of caption, my mother has
written: 'Known as Kacar Hasan, meaning "runaway"'. This,
I think, is not true, or at least partially true. To be a runaway,
the word would have to be kaçak – run away – or kaçan –
one who runs away. But, to be fair, I can't confirm that the
obverse is correct, that Hasan was indeed Qajar. But I did
grow up with my father repeating the sentiment that we were
distantly descended from Iranian royalty, brothers, which
made us little princes and princesses. Sometimes, with my
tongue in my cheek, I claim that I am one-sixteenth Iranian,
which I know to be a senseless statement, as if one can identify
with or as a nation-state. Fantasising about having once been
royalty is a not-uncommon working-class tendency, I think,
to entertain that one's lot in life is only a recent decline in
fortune, that we are nobler than this and maybe even above
it. I think about how it prevents communities from forming.
I won't fix up this house because I'm just about to move. I
won't get to know my neighbours because I won't be living
here for long. Not as exploited proletariat, but as temporarily
embarrassed millionaires. Or something more fatalistic: not
here for long – in heaven I'll get what's coming to me. Forget
about this one: in the next life I'll get what I deserved.

My father also describes the brothers as Uzun Hasan
and Uzun Hüseyin – Tall Hasan and Tall Hüseyin – because
royalty seemingly always possess superior physiques. This is
true only in fable, of course: Princess and the Pea, delicate-
featured, blond-haired and blue-eyed type of shit. We know
what happens in reality. I'm always having to remark that

inbreeding is the one thing that unites the very rich and the very poor. This is because, although I am not tall, I am a little inbred.

Tall Hasan is said to have brought with him from Iran much of his personal wealth. During the war, he is said to have buried the treasure somewhere in Çentik, intending to return for it, but in the end unable to do so. A series of displacements, huge population movements spurred by conflict and other demographic shifts, forced and accidental, meant that the Qajar fortune became lost. In Çentik, my father claims, such remnants of valuable possessions are often dug up – remains of Armenian and Kurdish homes even – alongside belongings they could never come back for, if they survived at all.

'Gerçek mi, değil mi merak ediyorum,' my father says.

He is in one of his rare chatty moods as we tour the backyard together. He is always shepherding me out into the garden as soon as I arrive at my parents' home, throwing down at my feet some slippers for me to put on and dashing off to point at things he has grown: hulking dragon fruit plants that have climbed and curled around an overhead trellis; planters of mint and basil that he raises for me in such excess that I drop every second pot off at friends' houses; neat, parallel rows of tomatoes, green capsicums and long green peppers prized by Turks and difficult to find here, and which he therefore sometimes donates by the bag to local kebab shops; lettuce that has gone wild and crops up in far-flung corners of the yard; and more experimental plants like blueberries, whose cultivation he is still getting the hang of, and potatoes, which grew almost by accident after he speculatively buried a few peels one day. He enjoys the way I don't know anything about growing my own food, and likes to giddily remark that it's easy, really. 'Köyde büyümenin sonucu,' he says. 'Siz şehirde büyüdünüz.' He grew up in a village and I didn't.

On a table in his backyard he has neatly lined up various repurposed empty pill bottles, now filled with bright red and yellow seeds and labelled: İSTANBUL BİBERİ, ANTALYA BİBERİ. He has his friends bring them back from their visits, but refuses to return to Turkey himself. He has no business going back, he often says, other than to perhaps one day find out where his mother is buried and to visit her grave. On this day, however, he expresses a second wish.

'I'd love to go back there with a metal detector and look around and dig. Just in case.'

It gives me a laugh to think of my father roaming the Turkish countryside with a metal detector strapped to his back, searching for hidden treasure the same way he has for all these years dug old coins out from underneath construction sites in Australia and kept them, cleaning them up and shining them with a kind of stray hope that one or a few will turn out to be valuable. He has shown me his coins a few times over the years, joking or perhaps believing that Mirasınıza kalır. I have perused them greedily, not because I think they have resale value, of course – I understand what the term mint condition signifies – but because I want him to feel valued and valuable.

I am not sure much of what appears on this piece of paper, which I have laminated and stuck to my office wall, is true. But fictive facts suit their purpose: an invented birthdate completes a section on a form, a fabricated last name tracks who has or has not paid their tithe or poll tax. The story of the lost fortune of Kacar Hasan functions as true for me, later, when I am reflecting on our interaction, because it reveals to me something about my father: that he often finds himself wondering at the question of why some end up poor and some end up rich.

Regarding the human preoccupation with discovering treasure, and the lore that surrounds it, Johannes Dillinger writes that 'vagabonds, that is, mostly very poor people, were regarded as experts in treasure. To a modern mind, this is exceedingly strange: if these vagrants knew so much about treasure and could deal with the treasure guardians, why did they not take the treasure for themselves? How could you be desperately poor and homeless while you had access to fabulous wealth?'

*

My father has only one photograph of his mother, which he squirrelled away from his eldest brother Ali's house in Narlıdere, and had blown up and sharpened, like a CIA agent in a tacky film – zoom, enhance, zoom, enhance – trying to press his forehead up against hers. Before he found the photo he had had no memory of her face. She died when he was five, on the table during a surgery to treat a respiratory illness that had plagued her her whole life. Ali had organised for her to receive this medical care, in the face of his father's protests, using a newfound class mobility made possible after he was deemed bright enough to move from the village and to study law in İzmir. I find myself thinking about this fact often – the way I also feel as if I have been plucked up and out, at random. I think about the way that the metaphor of the rose that grew from concrete has such a tight psychic grip on those who escaped poverty and go on to make art – it crops up often inside of Black hip hop and poetry, referencing Tupac Shakur. One interpretation of the image is that the rose has thrived in the most inhospitable of environments, a delicate and exceptional and highly unlikely thing. I am not just interested in roses but also in soil.

All the times their mother had been ill before this, my father's father had preferred instead to visit a cemevi and consult a dede, who would usually send my grandfather home with a muska in which a healing prayer was sealed. When my father's father had died – per the family tree, thirteen years after his mother – my father had finally been able to nose through the man's things, in particular to inspect the muskas, of which my grandfather had accrued tens, and which he kept stashed in a cabinet. My father explains to me that he probed them at first, poking them around with his finger and watching them jiggle and roll about on the shelf. After he did not instantly burst into flames, he felt emboldened to pick one up, profane and curious to understand how these objects could possess curative powers: he is an intuitive atheist, or alternately, this was his very last moment of faith. He unfurled one, unpicking the roll of paper inside to reveal its contents, wanting to know which long texts were written on their surface, but with the suspicion that they would come up entirely blank. He unfurled one more, and then another, and then he unfurled all of them, had all of their insides splayed open before him.

'Başından beri biliyordum zaten,' he says to me later. 'Annemi öldüren cahillik işte. Siz anlamazsınız.'

*

I learn about my father's third brother, Özer, only after he is shot and killed at point-blank range by two men, who put him on his knees on the side of a road in May of 2011. One of the men is Özer's brother-in-law. It comes out that Özer and his wife had been living apart for some months in the lead-up to the murder, that she had filed documents to divorce him, and alleged that he had vowed she would get nothing. It is obvious to all of us in the family that his wife is responsible and that she has promised her brother and his friend some portion of the proceeds of her inheritance in exchange for the murder.

It's hard to feel anything at all about the news when I hear it, given the blank spot on the family tree. I am trying to wrap my head around the fact that someone who we could describe as my uncle has been murdered in a conspiracy to steal his riches. It feels unreal, cinematic. I am not sad, but neither is my father.

'Ben de onu öldürmek istiyordum,' he says. 'O benden çok para çaldı. Ne ekersen onu biçersin.'

I learn that Özer was a wealthy businessman in Antalya. My father and Özer had run a framing business in İzmir before they became estranged. To my father it seems like poetic justice, that Özer was killed for his money. I hear whispers from the family that the story of what brought their business partnership to a close is more complicated than this, but I let it hang because it functions as true. *It was kill him or migrate to Australia,* he often says. *Kill him or come here.* Over the years I have heard innumerable stories about my parents' decision to relocate: for a higher standard of living; to escape the stigma of their Sunni–Alevi marriage; to escape my mother's parents. But this is a new one. Each narrative, when told, is relayed as if it were definitive. However, the stories often contradict each other: sometimes my father was tricked, promised a lucrative job and prosperity by my mother's brother, before being enlisted into gruelling, cheap, physically abusive and degrading manual work as the man's labourer. And sometimes it's this other one about Özer.

We tell ourselves stories, write short-hand synopses. I, for example, panic when I am asked questions about myself: how was your weekend? *I'm sorry, I don't know.* What did you get up to over Christmas? *Help me!* So I take to canning answers. My favourite movie is *A Serious Man,* and my favourite book is Kurt Vonnegut's *The Sirens of Titan.* These answers are true enough: they are both pieces of media I have revisited often, and drawn much solace from, since I was a teen. I think of them as companion texts, both to me and to each other.

A Serious Man tells the story of the middle-aged Larry, who, despite his anodyne nature – he is a good Jewish man, a good parent, a good husband, a decent brother – finds his life suddenly falling apart. His wife leaves him, his attempt to secure tenure at his institution is fettered, and he is blackmailed by a student. His faith is challenged by the sudden, undeserved reversal of fortune. Larry visits more than one rabbi, desperate to know what this terrible peripety signifies – is he cursed? – and they provide him with cryptic counsel. One tells an anecdote about a dentist who finds a meaningless message in a patient's teeth. When his brother is unexpectedly arrested, Larry tries to explain to the cops that it's all a mistake, there's been a mistake. Before the film ends, his luck swings back around: his wife's boyfriend dies; he gets tenure. And then as the film reaches its denouement, he receives a daunting phone call from a doctor hinting at a negative diagnosis, while a tornado roils across the landscape, ready to hit his town. Lady Philosophy's words in Boethius: the wheel spins. The high come down, the low ascend.

In *The Sirens of Titan,* a machine named Salo from the planet of Tralfamadore has been assigned a task. He is to convey a message from Tralfamadore to the other corner of the galaxy. The message is sealed and Salo is not allowed to ever open it. It becomes his key objective and his sole animus. The mission takes him over two hundred millennia, and his fellow Tralfamadorians sweep several unsuspecting humans into their machinations, part of a scheme to change the course of history for the sole purpose that a replacement machine part, which Salo needs to continue his journey, is built. The message finally arrives, and its content is revealed to be a single pinprick, a dot, which means, simply: *Greetings*.

Kill him or come here. If this explanation were true, then that would mean my father had, with much dignity and power, chosen to leave, rather than been tossed from one shore to another by some disinterested force.

Özer is remembered fondly by my cousin, Ali's daughter. When I visit Turkey in 2012, said cousin reports that she has been going to bed most evenings with Özer's case files splayed out in front of her on the bed, and falling asleep poring over them. The killers are being tried, but are mounting a peculiar defence narrative, aimed at mitigating the severity of their crime: they claim that while driving together, Özer had made a comment blaspheming, in some way, the prophet Mohammed and Allah, and as good Sunni men they could not stand for it. They were so riled up over it that they could not wait, had to stop the car, pull him aside and kill him with the shotgun they had brought. When I try to make it make sense to my friends here, I take to describing it as the *Alevi panic defence*. Although the two men are imprisoned, Özer's widow nearly gets away, but because the Günaydın assets are frozen by the state, she does not pay the killers the money she has promised them and their families. So they confess her involvement in the murder, and finally she is imprisoned in 2013. The story makes headlines, and as I search for more information – during this online trawl I find and save to my computer a photograph of my uncle, the first one I have ever seen, and I contemplate Sharpie-ing him onto the family tree, but what claim do I have to him really? –

I grow used to reading the same phrase over and over. Serveti için öldürüldü: he was killed for his fortune.

*

At lunch, Tex asks me how it feels to be the first generation in my family to have healed from decades of trauma and poverty and earned enough money to be able to offer a good life to my hypothetical children. We are sitting in the sun under a rickety cafe umbrella, staring out onto the university oval, winding down and preparing to ease into the summer. Tex is about to submit his thesis – we are both PhD candidates in the same department, and have grown close as friends – and although I have not achieved anything nearing this, I am feeling idle and languorous too.

I designate 2020 my 'flop era'. I'm sick of producing hits. I decided this after I found myself remarking to Justin one evening, as we were lying in bed, both spent from the indignities of the day, holding hands side-by-side like two teens in a disaster movie staring into a chasm that has opened up in the earth, that I can understand why sometimes people drive themselves into lakes – the immense burden, the pressure. Afterwards, I decide I'd like to minimise times in my life when I am a person who believes that statement. I make the resolution that every year my resolution is going to be to work less, now that I have achieved escape velocity. The years between 2015 and 2019 I tore my arse in two, worked two or three jobs and sixty-hour weeks and took shit work and justified it all by reminding myself that my father worked seven days a week for thirteen hours a day for thirty years, and that, therefore, to walk around a shop with a roof over my head, or to sit and type at a computer, is nothing by comparison. I feel, although this turns out to be comically untrue, as if no one can take away from me my partner, my home, my reputation in my chosen field, my career successes. I've been tapped as a lucky recipient of one of those good lives. So I believe it's time to cruise, that is, work only as hard as everyone else does and not harder.

I take to having real lunches. Nominally I am meant to be learning how to relax, but I have a knack for diverting conversations towards trauma. Tex asks me the question after he probes a little and we discuss our childhoods. I like him: we seem to match each other in our level of stridency. Justin hated that I love to argue, and I learned, during our relationship, how to speak to him in the way he would like to be spoken to. He often said that I was so fixed and firm in my beliefs, sure I was right until I found out I was wrong, and then capitulated so fast it gave him whiplash. I used to ask him what the alternative would be: to start off doubting (they teach women to doubt themselves, you know), or to dig in my heels and never concede? I'm not married to my beliefs – I just want to get to the bottom of the matter at hand. Justin used to say he believed in a healthy level of agnosticism, and that if I'm not married we should probably change that.

I'm not saying that the shouting matches Tex and I sometimes hold in our shared office are a good thing. Only that it's hard to find someone you can yell at.

I think Tex's question is both right and wrong. I tell him, 'I think that if I have achieved some measure of healing, that's amazing, but maybe it's overly self-congratulatory. I'm more inclined to believe that if I can provide a better life for the generation after me, it's not because of anything I've done, really. It's mostly because I started off with less trauma.'

My psychologist once hedged this theory. For most of the sessions during our first year together, this had been a sticking point. I found myself repeating versions of the same question: why me? Who am I to be okay? Why shouldn't I follow – why aren't I following – the trajectory of others in my family? I'm not special, am I? If I'm okay, that would make me special, no? I must either not be okay, make myself not okay, or I must be special. Survivor's guilt makes you believe simultaneously that you are the best and the worst person alive. What's crucial is that you feel unlike anyone else that exists, fundamentally marked out as in but not of this world. But my psychologist is always talking me off ledges of imputed meaning.

'If you're more okay than anyone else ... Well, look, it's possibly because your parents paid less attention to you,' she once remarked. I laughed, finding the statement darkly comic – attracted to what felt like her callousness.

'True,' I demurred. 'She once said my oldest sister was a much bigger investment than me, that losing her was more serious, that she still had me but it was worth less.'

'Well, then,' she said. 'So she paid less attention to you, which means she could inflict less damage. And you said you read a lot?'

I nodded. 'Right, yeah. I mostly sat in the corner and read. They were well and truly over having children by

then. Or over each other, anyway. And I am the youngest –
quantitatively, there's less time in which I could have gotten
fucked up.'

'So,' she says, 'it seems to me that you don't have to be
like them because you are not them.'

I remember rushing out in a daze, containing a rising
giddiness, after this session. When I arrived home, I remember collapsing backwards onto my bed with my shoes on,
almost as if returning home thrilled about a good date, the
world unfurling before me. The relief made me giggle – the
discovery that I am average, so average, and not marked to
save anyone, nor capable of doing so. It was just luck. Pure
dumb luck. I kept muttering it to myself: luck. Luck! Ha!
Thank fuck!

'I'll tell you one thing,' I say. Tex goes to snag a wedge
from me and I edge my plate closer to him. 'That thing people
say sometimes along the lines of, *I'm going to heal my family,
I'm going to heal my bloodline. I'm going to lift the curse.* That's
nothing. Or at least, you can't heal the ones that came before
you. We can't do anything nearing that.'

Tex throws down the other half of the wedge in disgust,
and I pretend to bristle – you dare discard one of these
cosmically delicious potatoes? – and we pretend to bicker
until it's time to go back to work.

I really do stridently believe this, although there are times
I wonder who I am trying to convince. Later, I find myself
issuing the same diatribe to another colleague, Kyle, a man
I woefully only began paying attention to after he revealed
himself to possess working class credentials that outstrip

mine. He had originally tripped my yuppie radar, I tell him later, as if he should be flattered I am bothering now to give him the time of day. I explain it is a filtering system I apply to colleagues, designed on paper to preserve my energy, but which in reality means I am sometimes hostile for no reason to people I have plenty in common with, especially given that we are all always hiding our true selves in institutions, and that I, Eda, would not pass my own test these days.

He and I once sat in the shared office, both working late, both dealing with high workloads made necessary by financial stressors that mean we are the only ones remaining after others have left, and I unpacked my theory about luck, and then did my usual song and dance venting about the over-representation of high-income earners in the student body of my university, which rivals that of Ivy Leagues and Oxbridge. Kyle has a tendency to say 'It's all good' and 'I've accepted it'. Once, he sheepishly admitted that he sometimes visualises a duffel bag in his mind into which he shoves negative thoughts and memories. I often insist that he should be madder, as if it's me who's the right level of angry. On this occasion, I said, gently, 'You don't need to say everything is good all the time, you know,' and he responded, staring at the sun setting behind the clouds through the window overlooking Parramatta Road, 'But it *is* good, you know, that the students have had an all right time through life. Earlier, when we were talking about luck, you said you had to believe that because that was the only way you could make peace with things. It must be nice, you know, not to have anything to have to make peace with. You can just go.'

*

Bananas came to Çentik a handful of years before the moon landing and a handful after the American president had his head blown off. The family crowded around the table was not sure how to eat them. Muhammet's father floated that maybe you fry them up, add onion. It looked like a vegetable, after all. Ali abi had left them on the table on his way out, but failed to proffer instructions.

Ali was going to be a judge. On his visit he had kneeled down and looked Muhammet and Özer level in the face and told them he would bring Muhammet and his other abi to İzmir soon, then walked headlong out the door. Muhammet was convinced the man was a stranger or an extra-terrestrial: he wore slacks and a button-down shirt and a necktie, and he demanded they all sit quietly at the dinner table and use their manners. He had hit Muhammet over the head, repeatedly, when Muhammet had failed to quieten down over dinner the night before. Years later, a doctor would ask him if he'd ever burst an eardrum.

'Go to your grandmother's house,' his father barked at Muhammet. 'She's a good cook.'

Muhammet snapped one off, running down the dirt path with the banana held aloft.

'Babaanne, babaanne,' he trilled, chasing up the stairs and catching her braced out the window hanging a pastel yellow sheet out to dry.

'Ne var?' she said, turning, and he showed her what he was holding.

'Bu nedir, babaanne? Nasıl yenmeli? Ali abi bize bıraktı.'

Her grandmother took the fruit from his hand, inspecting it for a few moments, then wrapped her thumb and fist around the upper pointy segment and pulled. She then broke off half of the off-white inside and handed it over.

'Pişirmeye hiç gerek yok. It's a fruit. Like an orange.'

Muhammet jammed the thing into his mouth, wolfed it down stringy parts and all.

'Sağol, babaanne,' he called, racing back with the peel clutched in his fist as evidence.

He arrived back, huffing, and noticed that there were four bananas left on the table. He knew there were six of them gathered around, and that the bananas would have to be split. Most likely his portion would be zero. Gingerly, he reached up and took one into his hand, snapped off the pointed bit as his grandmother had demonstrated. He knew, intellectually, that he would be beaten if he ate the thing.

Here is how the ruse went:

'Böyle yenir. Önce soyuyorsun. First, you peel it.'

He peeled it. They observed, holding still, and it gave him enough time to mash as much of the fruit into his mouth as he could. It was not a ruse, not really. He couldn't stop himself.

They beat him after all, and did not give him anything to eat for a day and a half, after which time the bananas were all gone. He did not see bananas again until two years later, after Ali abi made good on his promise. İzmir was the first place he'd ever seen an electric light switch. He had Ali turn the light on and then off and then on again before he could grasp what was happening, believe that it was not some trick of the light or büyü.

'Can you believe such ignorance?' he asks his daughter later. 'Cahillik işte. It's a disease with no cure.'

*

My father's Ahmet amca died on his back in Çentik. The men from the neighbourhood rushed to Ahmet's house, at first attempting to revive him. My father was five at the time, or thereabouts; his true birthdate is not known, although we celebrate it in March. My father's father only grunted when they came around yelling for Küçük Muhammet, and gestured that he join the men outside. Muhammet leapt away from the heater, where he had been standing on his tiptoes stirring a pot, preparing dinner, and joined the men.

The men had him march double-time to match their long strides, leaving him with only a moment to cast one glance back at his house. It was unevenly plastered, some of the mudbrick still visible and in other places cracked. His mother thought the house was two hundred and fifty years old. Serving as its fence were crooked branches nailed together to form posts, and its wall was made of flat rocks piled atop one another, as tall as Muhammet.

'Ahmet amcan vefat etti,' they explained, and pointed.

In the orchard, Muhammet sat down next to the corpse cross-legged. He wiggled his hand down in between the dust and the dead man's cooling skin to reach into his pocket. Jagged little rocks grazed the back of his hand, embedded themselves into the webbing of his fingers. It took him a long time to retrieve the man's house keys.

That's how my father came to touch a corpse – or something along those lines. My father tells me this story fifty-five years later, introducing it by declaring, 'I have touched a dead body twice.' My father says, his eyes wide and excited, 'I bet you've never even *seen* a corpse. Right? Right? Our lives are so different.'

I nod hard, and listen with my mouth slightly open, committed to documenting both stories. But by chance I only remember one, because the image sticks with me, of the little hand wriggling into the slit of fabric, with the sun beating down. Sweat on his brow, running into his pristine cow eyes, with their long eyelashes. I have my father's eyes – but not really.

*

In Narlıdere, 2012. We'd been sleeping on the floor of my uncle and aunt's living room. My ninety-five-year-old great aunt kept vigil over us, checking if we needed anything, fluffing our blankets at night. They knew that, where I'm from, it never gets as cold as it does in İzmir in winter. Before bed they showed me photo after photo of my father when he was younger – standing cross-armed and back-to-back with friends, or posing in the İspanyol paça pants for which he is remembered by relatives he has never come back to see. At home, my mother often remarks, 'You didn't think he always dressed so shit, did you? No, that's only after we got here' – as well as ones he doesn't have, and others that they don't know that he has. Out of shyness, all I could say was, on repeat, çok komik, which they, in turn, thought was funny.

Back home my mother mocks the frugality of my father's side of the family. But it's hard earned. When my father was shuffled from home to home that couldn't provide for him, and beaten in lieu of being fed, it was sometimes by the same aunt whose floor I slept on in 2012. When he recounts these facts to me now, my father bears no ill will, and only holds out his palms and asks, rhetorically, 'Ne yapabilirdi ki? On altı yaşındaydı ve yeni evliydi. Nasıl bana bakacaktı?'

As a child, some nights he would lie awake on the ground floor of the house in the köy, where no one slept, waiting to hear the sound of an orange falling out of a tree onto the ground in the orchard in the back, so he could creep out and claim it. My mother tells this story frequently, with great pity. Neither parent wastes food – what doesn't get eaten is scattered into the backyard so that the birds can have some. My father's father would, I have been told, never place food on the ground, not even for the animals. Food for a bird might be placed on a branch instead, elevated.

'Bunlar nimet,' he would say.

I think about how odd I used to find it to be raised believing that to let bread fall to the floor was a sin, thinking that it was a superstition rather than an act with moral or immoral content. The last time my father reminisced about his father this way, I countered by describing how I had recently microwaved six cobs of corn, intending to eat them one evening, but become distracted by some long work task, and found them the next morning dried out and wrinkled where I had left them. And then I had tossed them directly in the trash. Neither parent could quite believe it: I wanted to explain it was the result of a generational divide, maybe, or neoliberalism, something to do with being particularly time-poor. *Time-poor is the new poor!* – hah.

My father left Çentik when he was young, part of a large migration of rural Turks to cities which set up gecekondu neighbourhoods on their skirts. This is a common pattern in large metropolises, and is paralleled in countries such as Brazil and India: the attempt to execute a centrally planned, organised city inevitably gives rise to an informal and generally working-class periphery, one which must exist in order to make the centre function, because it supplies that centre with its labour, its sociality and its politics. Val Plumwood calls them shadow places, Robert Neuwirth shadow cities. Ali started a housing cooperative in the Narlıdere gecekondu. The street I was on in 2012 bears his name for this reason, and he has helped many Alevis to own homes.

Turkey's Alevis are said to adhere to principles abstracted out from Islam, not of zakat, per se, but something more material like mutual aid, and they helped lead the radical leftist and communist surges of the sixties. In İstanbul, the gecekondu neighbourhood of Nurtepe was built, physically planned and then built up, by revolutionary leftists, who even expropriated cables and electricity poles from the state to give the suburb its power. The organisers then compiled lists of the poor in need of housing, and then gave them homes. In Turkey, entire neighbourhoods can be Alevi-majority, which sometimes means that they are left neighbourhoods. In towns like İstanbul's 1 Mayıs (named after Labour Day), Gazi, Okmeydanı and Armutlu, they kick out cops, organise armed militia resistance to fascists. They are spaces that would be unrecognisable to my mother, who is descended from a smattering of Grey Wolves, and whose father is said to have died from a heart attack, cigarette hanging from his lips, in front of the television, because he was so furious that the right hadn't performed as well as he'd hoped in the 1987 Turkish general election. This is how I know that neighbourhoods can be your home, but not nation-states, for the latter is fictive: far too abstracted, zoomed out, to speak to these local vicissitudes.

I imagine my father as one of these communists. I appraise in a new light that, for all my Marxist learning at school, the first person to ever name capitalism, to teach me the word, was my father. One of his favourite phrases, which Justin and I knew to mouth along to, such is the frequency with which he repeats it, is one that we noticed he inevitably declares after we have lamented some shitty thing or another: 'That's capitalism,' he says. With an air of resignation: 'All part of the game.' Justin loved to imitate him, 'That's kapita-lizm!' When my father says it, it's not an endorsement but nor is it always a critique. It's another way of saying 'that's just the way it is'. It makes me think about Sara Ahmed, who identifies fatalism not as a neutral position, but as taking the side of nothing changing.

Still, my father has never made much money as a brick-layer, intentionally, choosing instead to trade favours. He'll build you a retaining wall if he can call upon you to fix his leaking tap some time, or to give him a container of the raw honey that he likes, or tip him off about where to find wild greengages just outside of Sydney.

*

I admit it, I don't know my father well. I am sketching him restlessly, attempting to capture his likeness, although he won't sit still. Taking shortcuts, resorting to shallow renderings. Growing up, he was always halfway out of the room, leaving the table during family functions after shortly eating a meal to sit out back and chain-smoke by himself. So I read into small things: that he shares all the revolutionary content that he sees on Facebook, videos about Mahir Çayan and Deniz Gezmiş, songs from Grup Yorum, videos about the revolutionary and lawyer Ebru Timtik, killed by the state. This is how I have scaffolded him out, perhaps in contraposition to my mother; I got my best traits from my father. We're both lefties. He's basically an agrarian socialist. I'm carrying on the torch, you know. But I don't know. When he shows me a photograph of himself in the eighties, he has a full moustache. In Turkey, during this period, communists wore their moustaches long and the right-wingers wore them neat and cropped and rectangular. I goad my mother with it: look, you married an Alevi *and* a commie. But on this day my father insists he just did what everyone else did; there was a social expectation among his circle that they all have one like this, that's all. On this day he insists that he is not now nor has he ever been a communist. Another time he says he stopped believing all of that once he got here, and all the fight went out of him. It's possible he doesn't mean what he says, that he was in a bad mood one or both of those days. It's possible he's three-dimensional: believing one thing in one moment, another in another. But it's also possible that I am searching for a likeness that is not there.

I am afraid of this, because to acknowledge it would be to acknowledge all the things we do not have in common. Sometimes I prefer to retreat into the comfort of the fantasy, which makes it easy to think of him during the course of my day and feel uncomplicated fondness. Other times I force myself to confront the ways that we disappoint each other. Once, he commented that boys are smarter than girls – they all do better in tests. I wondered why he was bothering to invest so much time in my education if he believed that; what was the point of him driving me to my selective school in the Hills, or to my debating meet-ups. At the time I tried to remind him that poverty is what prevents girls from going to or staying in school, and not a natural difference in aptitude. He remarked that he had also grown up in poverty, that as the youngest boy this is the same reason he had not been able to do further study beyond high school, despite his smarts.

I try to patronise him again, once, after he complains about a family member. He says, 'Koskoca adam. Okumuş, eğitim görmüş biri. Evi var, köyü var. O mutlu değilse biz ne yapacağız?' I conclude that he is stretching his materialism a little far, assuming that the only necessary ingredients for a good life are a home, an education and an income. Or, he is trying to protect himself from the dark knowledge that you can provide for someone's physical needs, and that it still might not be enough, can't heal every wound. I try to reason with him and explain that they are unwell, and that not even money and an education can fix that. If they could be happy, they would be, wouldn't they? He responds that he himself has been sad for a long time, sick in the head for a long time. He has carried his sadness with him everywhere he goes, his longest companion and oldest friend. I remind myself that it is impossible to see others when you have never felt seen.

Once, at Hungry Jack's – one of those meals gorged upon as if post-marathon, for we have just finished the two-person job of taking my mother to a doctor's appointment – he revealed that he always knew about my mother. I had been wondering if he loved her in a way that made him unable to code her behaviours as emotional abuse. But, he said, he had had to make the choice to save himself, to protect himself, when staring down the barrel of their life together. So he left us alone with her. And all I could possibly say, all I could make myself say, was, 'Well, maybe you shouldn't have,' and I took my dignity and my bags of fast food and walked out and back to the car, thinking to myself, *I'm the child, I was the child, I'm the child.*

Another time, also in the car, he gave me a hard time about not messaging or calling my mother enough. During this period, he chidingly began referring to me as 'Fortnightly', trying to make the nickname stick – referring to the (in)frequency of my visits, attempting to jokingly shame me into trying to make this unhappy person happy, something I gave up on long ago. He calls me when he is at the end of his rope, in order to hand the phone off quickly to her, knowing that I will answer his calls but I won't always answer hers. Sometimes the calls come back to back: my mother's I ignore, and his I answer after two or three rings. I want to feel guilty about it.

When he says that I'm lucky to have a mother, that he didn't have one, and then asks me if I love her, I just respond, 'I love you, Dad.' When I arrive at the house on a visit, he is quick to leave the room, abscond to the garden. Sometimes he'll remark that he's leaving us alone in order to let us *gossip and catch up,* as if that is ever what occurs. In reality, my mother has told me things she has never told him.

In the car, after he called me 'Fortnightly' one time too many, my voice cracked when I said, 'Büyürken ben baktım ona. Ben annelik ettim.'

Later, I ask my therapist if he is actually a bad person. She tells me she doesn't think there are bad people, just bad coping mechanisms. Desperate people do desperate things; to always do the right thing is a luxury. If the people in your life have always been sweet and good to you, that is the definition of luck indeed. I repeat this mantra: no bad people, just bad coping mechanisms. For one of my key leftist beliefs to hold any water at all, I must believe that this is true, that we mustn't just 'cancel' others, that almost everyone, provided with the right circumstances, can change and move through processes of accountability and amends, and that the worst things we've done in our lives should not define us forever.

My next therapy appointment is held on Skype due to the pandemic, and I raise the subject again, after I have failed again to do some task for my mother that my father requests of me, and which he deems a failure of compassion when I say no, and which I consider to be a violation of boundaries. I'm angry at someone I want to only feel good things about: selfish. My therapist asks, 'Why does his opinion matter so much to you?'

I conclude that I want a parent. I'm greedy for a parent: that's the way we are most alike.

We hit minute sixty, and she wraps us up, doing what she always does, and asks, 'So what are you going to do?' Really, I'm giving therapy to myself. That's her secret. I am the scarecrow and the lion and the power was in me all along. I ruminate for a few moments, for once at a loss. And then I say, 'I am going to accept that nothing I do will ever be enough,' and I watch my own face in the monitor while I weep for seven unbilled minutes.

*

When Muhammet was twelve he stood in the village square, the rough block of land on which the villagers congregated to gossip and banter. It was a few steps outside the village hall, outside which, on a bright and long day, a table would be set up and the women would spice and roll endless raw meatballs. For this reason, the village's most popular stray dog could be found lying on his side in the square, eyeballing passers-by, languidly sniffing to assess if they had any meat for him.

On this night Muhammet was trying to hide with the benefit of the darkness. Before his father had rolled up demanding to know where he was, he had been eavesdropping on the men in the square who stood discussing the fact that the Americans had just sent a man to the moon.

'İşe yaramaz oğlum nerede? Hm?'

His friend Kemal said, loudly, trying to divert his father's attention, speaking as if inviting him to join in on a grand joke: 'Bilmiyorum, Seyit amca. I don't know, Uncle Seyit. I don't know. Haven't seen him. Seyit amca, biliyor musun? Did you know that the first person walked on the moon? I heard it on the radio. When the Americans arrived, when they arrived, do you know what aydede did? Aydede grabbed his baston in his hand and chased and beat them with it till they ran away.'

He asks his daughter if she knows who aydede is and she nods.

The oldest man to be in the square this evening remarked, 'Iyi yapmış. Good on him.' He was not joking; he had genuinely taken this myth as fact and easily believed that there was a man living on the moon who had waved his stick at the Americans, and beaten them over the head with it for intruding. Possibly something the man would have done himself, were he the custodian of the moon.

'İnanıyor musun?' he asks his daughter. 'Can you believe it? Cahillik, işte. Pure ignorance. With all your education you probably can't even conceive of someone being so cahil.'

*

134

When we were both younger, my father maintained a working tape deck in his ute, along with a collection of tapes. My mother called him our ATM and our chauffeur. He paid bills and drove us around. We didn't speak much – on some occasions he might launch into a story – and generally would listen to Turkish radio on SBS, or to a cassette. My father favours the Alevi aşıks, poets who put their poems over saz music, like, in western terms, minstrels, bards or troubadours. The music covers the usual themes – love, religion and mysticism, nature. But my father can't stand the spiritual ones. Another common reprise of his: if there is a God, then why did it kill his mother? Onun günahı neydi? So we listen to those that deal with earthlier matters: poverty, the inevitability of suffering, death.

We like Âşık Veysel, who was from Sivas like my father. I remember him explaining, when I was very young, that smallpox had sent Veysel blind in his childhood. After Veysel devoted his life to mastering the bağlama, and then accrued much acclaim and recognition as an artist, he was offered a medical operation that could reverse his condition. Although his poetry often compares blindness to exile, something that plunged him into a state of separation setting him intractably and forever apart from others, Veysel declined the offer. He had become attached and accustomed to his blindness. That's the way the myth about the blind bard goes: through his lack of it, the bard accesses a different and more profound sight. My father remarked that he found that beautiful.

I listen to Veysel's most famous song, 'Uzun İnce Bir Yoldayım', over and over, and imagine myself and my father treating life like a long, thin, winding road, which we must traverse, without knowing why we continue. At my most miserable I find myself remarking that if life is a game I am just trying to beat all the levels and get to the end. It's not even his favourite song. I infiltrate the Çentik Facebook group without my father's knowledge. I take to smoking in the backyard of my Petersham home, and when my father visits I close the door on his face, rush to the back to hide the ashtray and dump the butts into the bin before I let him in.

My father's favourite song is by Aşık Gülabi, called 'Beş Nüfusa Bir Tek Ekmek'. I am compelled to translate it:

> There's a trouble in my soul
> That won't leave me alone
> Poverty is a plague
> Leave me, I say, but still it's here
>
> I'm wondering how to get by
> I don't know where to go
> One piece of bread for a family of five
> Let it be enough, I beg, but it does not suffice

There's a small photo, the only one of my father as a child, sitting on the countertop in my parents' kitchen. It was taken at school, I think, and is in sepia – he is about six. When I see it for the first time, I understand why my family claims I bear his likeness. I grew up hearing the phrase 'Baban gibi

sarışınsın', but our skin tones don't match. Mine is the result
of years spent indoors variously reading, socialising online,
studying, and working at a university, like a goldfish that
turns white because its bowl has been kept in a windowless
room. His is the result of years building homes under the
Australian sun, not even once wearing sunscreen, despite
having had at least one skin cancer cut out of his body. He
fails to mitigate risk constantly. We ask him to wear a helmet
if he is going to climb a ladder, secure himself if he's going
to ascend some scaffolding. He enjoys telling the story of
the time he fell from a height and sustained a head injury,
emerging from unconsciousness an indeterminate amount
of time later and taking himself to the hospital. In running
his own business all these years, he has never paid himself
superannuation. When I ask him what his plans are for
retirement, he says they are to die.

In this particular photo, though, the one in which he is
six years old, my father is genuinely fair, his hair sandy and
his face pale. He looks miserable.

*

For most of my second year in therapy I take to feeling numb.
My psychologist takes away from me my high highs and
my low lows; in other words, she helps me to emotionally
regulate, and it feels terrible. Rather, it feels like nothing. My
diet of neutral, proportionate emotions feels like making the
passage from choofing down fat cigars to chewing sugar-free
unflavoured gum, the kind called Falım, sold in Turkey and
that comes wrapped in a little piece of paper from which

you read your fortune: it is bland and I am in withdrawal. I go from always being a one or a ten to floating perpetually between a three and a seven. I think often that you could ram a cattle prod into my thigh and I'd feel nothing, I'm so fucking regulated.

Moments that once might have felt heady, unbearably intense, fade to a dull drone. Ruminations that used to feel essential I get to the bottom of – why me? Am I a bad person? What's the right thing to do? – have been replaced by nothing at all, a kind of psychic silence. I carefully prune out of existence every unhelpful thought – he doesn't deserve this; I pity him; I hate myself; maybe it's his fault, he shouldn't have done that; why can't she just ...; if she wanted a different outcome she should have done something different; if he wanted me to show up he should have been a better father – that precedes acceptance and I go straight to acceptance. My colleague Kyle and I are mindless-mindful automatons programmed for acceptance: new acceptance target acquired. Beep, beep: acceptance processing complete. There doesn't need to be a reason why it's this way; it just is this way. The attempt to apportion blame, or assign guilt – to myself or others – is an attempt to make it make sense. But it doesn't. If I were religious, I could believe that I had a surplus of grace: a gift granted to me from on high that I don't deserve and do not merit. This is one of the 'good Gs' I have been encouraged by my therapist to cultivate, alongside generosity and gratitude. 'There but for the grace of God' kind of shit that tells me to acknowledge my gifts, to say thank you, ya şükür, and send it all back out into the world.

The next week I say no to my father again and it goes down easier: he takes on the burden instead. It's not what I wanted. I can't help but think of him for a moment as a saint. Gözlerinden öpüyorum, baba: a sort of reverent Turkish way of relating to our elders I can't usually muster. I catch myself, though, because I want not to idealise my parents, to grant them a fuller range of humanity than that.

My mother always repeated the mantra that cennet annelerin ayakları altındadır. But of her own mother she once said to me, 'Havadan ağzımla kuş tutsam yaranamazdım.' Even if I were to catch a bird out of the air in my mouth I couldn't have satisfied her, which I replay in my mind over and over. But still she crawled, and crawled, after her, my mother said, in a way that we don't crawl after her. She was so disappointed, and I couldn't tell if it was in herself or me.

I keep getting ready to look back on my parents' lives – I am eulogising them pre-emptively. I get ready to make myself believe that there is no migrant success story and no neat meaning that makes it all click into place, and no way that my success, such as it is, could make it all have been worth it, given how little of it had to do with me. Therefore, they will go down in history as two people who just got their arses fucking kicked and battered by life, and it's sort of their fault and sort of not, and it's not mine. They came into my life pre-crushed by gargantuan forces like capitalism and patriarchy and brutal physical violence that proved insurmountable. To believe I could do anything about it would be grandiose, one of my therapist's two designated 'unhelpful Gs', alongside guilt.

Although I won't be revising my canned answers any time soon, I do have a new favourite film, called *Kelebekler*. It tells the story of three city-dwelling siblings, two brothers and a sister, two living in Turkey and another in Germany, who must reunite to go on a long road trip because their estranged father has passed away in the village of Hasanlar. The siblings are not close, because there is too much baggage from their childhoods between them, which casts a pall over their relationship-that-could-have-been. They go back to Hasanlar to bury their father. 'Just bury him already,' one of the siblings screams hysterically towards the end of the film, over the dead man's grave, because her brothers won't stop arguing. Just bury him, just bury him. Their father has, in his will, directed the siblings to pay a visit to a blind shepherd, whom they meet under a tree in the film's concluding scene, wending their way to the edge of the village and sitting by his feet, awaiting a story. Falteringly, the shepherd explains that the siblings' father had offered him shelter from heavy rain one day many years ago. Their father had been generous enough to provide the blind shepherd with a meal, and when the house's roof started to leak, the shepherd had climbed up there and repaired it. 'So, in sum … ', says the shepherd. They hold their breath, waiting. 'You owe me 500 lira.' The siblings stare dumbfounded for a few moments. But then they begin to laugh. And they climb up onto their feet, and they walk away. My favourite Erkut Taçkın song, 'Baba' – Dad – plays them out.

*

My father doesn't gamble and he doesn't drink – wouldn't even let a rum ball pass his lips if it were on offer – but he used to play the lotto and he does smoke. The smoking, he says, is the one release he should be allowed to have: he deserves something. I repeat this now, ironically, when my friends get on my case about smoking. I deserve a little something, don't I? Please just let me have my poisoned treat.

As a child I used to fantasise about winning a lotto draw: how I would redistribute my winnings, mentally apportioning a million to each immediate family member, and then giving the rest away to charity. The fantasy scratched the same itch as prayer, which I also used to do, until I turned twelve and became sure I was an atheist, a conviction that has now softened as I realise how grandiose it is to believe I can be sure about anything. Before that, though, every night I would sit up and recite the meaningless Arabic I had committed to memory by rote – Bismillah al-rahman al-rahim … ashhadu an la ilaha illallah wa ashhadu anna Muhammadan abduhu wa rasuluh – and then wish in English for health and happiness for me and my family.

Sociologists have found that the poor spend more on lottery tickets than the wealthy. To explain this puzzle, they have posited a constellation of possible causes, which vary from socialisation (peer effects), to optimism (hey, maybe), to fatalism (a belief that their lives are controlled by factors outside of their control). Aren't they?

Throughout my postgraduate studies I've taught a variety of classes on politics, international relations and political theory. The structure–agency problem always comes up, so I work out a routine for how to teach it. I pose some controversial scenario, like if in a patriarchal society – which most societies on earth are – a man grows up to be sexist, to hold misogynistic views, is he the by-product of large structural factors outside of his control, or are we just making excuses for him? Is it in his power to change, to make better decisions? My students give me a smattering of responses: yes, he can change. The structures we are inside of are not entirely invisible – we can become alive to them and exercise some power within them. If people were incapable of exercising agency, then there would be zero good men, right? That's the 'acting in a tight spot' theory. Or they say, yes, some people can change, but we must remember that not everyone can exercise the same amount of agency over their lives, depending on who has access to more privilege or more resources. To that I respond, 'Yes, definitely. Some people have more agency than others.' And then I wait for a student to complete the tableau and say, no, I think structures determine much more than we give them credit for: they decide who we become, we can't always just individualistically fight our way through. That's when I end the discussion, and remark something blasé, like 'And that's the structure–agency problem, folks!'

But in reality I am haunted by the question of what the bounds of structure, agency, luck and privilege are. Sometimes I exculpate my mother entirely, concluding that if she could be some other way, then she would be, and that I might behave exactly the same if I'd experienced what she had. Then I decide I am being patronising in keeping my expectations so low, and erasing the successful efforts and hard work of those who have experienced violent things and still transformed their lives, made good decisions and exercised enough agency not to reproduce cycles of abuse. In other words, if we're all fated to forever be the way that we are, then we cannot explain why any two people who experience identical conditions go on to be two different ways. Researchers make the argument that one of the key factors that affects a kid's ability to make it through infelicitous life circumstances is a quality called an internal locus of control, that affects how actively or passively they move through their lives.

But then I fret that to argue this would be to agree with the bootstrap narrative, which I see crop up in writing about the working class again and again. At the airport recently I caught a glimpse of a paperback memoir about working class America: the author 'beat the odds' through a little hard work, unlike the rest of his relatives (played, in the filmic adaptation, by Glenn Close) who are poor addicts caught in the throes of what the author describes as learned helplessness. But that's not what odds are and it's not how they work. Personal pluckiness is not, and can never be, enough to overcome the weight of structures, to turn a game of chance – or better yet, a game that is rigged – into a game of skill.

Before my 'flop era', I was obsessed with achievements. However, none of them ever felt like success, never felt quite sufficient to cure my abiding feelings of precarity and worthlessness. People used to tell me to be proud of my accomplishments, such as they are, and I am, but I am also firmly of the belief that they are, in important ways, unearned. Merit is a myth, I remind friends, who I know only want me to be proud of myself. But I must believe that if the terrible things that befall, for example, the poor, aren't deserved, then nothing good that happens is deserved, either. I see meritocratic thinking too often overtake acquaintances and peers who have grown up poor, and met with an irreconcilable cognitive dissonance when it comes time to answer the question of why they got out when someone else did not. I see them start to think to themselves, well, I must just be incredible, amazingly hard-working. But I can't believe that. If hard work were the answer, then the single mother of three who works eighty hours a week at three menial jobs should be wealthy and Jeff Bezos should be dead. I therefore must believe that if I, for example, am successful in finding a new job, it's not because I'm better than the other candidates, but rather that it is a lottery and they may as well have drawn our names out of a hat. Or if I am successful in, for example, a grant application, it's not because I am especially clever or talented, but rather that I am leveraging the privilege and education I have that makes me adept at expressing myself in ways that institutions value. Justin and I made sure to always check one another if we got too down about rejections we experienced in our careers – making the mistake of assuming that these rejections said something about our worth and not about the cosmic randomness of the universe – using the shorthand: 'Ecclesiastes 9/11.'

Still, sometimes I try to quantify what I think is the unique blend of control I think any of us possess: talent or merit or hard work are worth 10 per cent, perhaps, privilege 45 per cent, and luck another 45 per cent. On one hand I know that it's vital to cede control over outcomes, for my sanity, but not so much so that I won't at least hit the brakes if I see another car approaching. I don't want to just roll over, but I don't want to always feel hypervigilant either, like my success is entirely up to me, like if I fail, or someone treats me poorly, or I find myself broke one day, then I am entirely to blame for not simply being better, faster, stronger, waking up earlier in the day and going to bed later at night. So I circle round to accepting that if something terrible happens I wouldn't have been able to stop it and it won't have been my fault. That line from *The Sirens of Titan* comes back to me: 'I was a victim of a series of accidents, as are we all.' But some of us are more victim than others. I circle down these drains endlessly, vacillate between accepting that I am nothing and brainstorming ways to be more.

*

In his foreword to the 2018 edition of the *Communist Manifesto*, Yanis Varoufakis writes that, 'For a manifesto to succeed, it must speak to our hearts like a poem.'

Underneath Varoufakis' Manifesto on the Manifesto, I write my own, shittier manifesto, making a nesting doll of manifestoes. I write, 'We don't love our lives enough to want to save them, or to want one for others. We need to restore to the social world relations other than class relations (smiley face). To seek joy is a political responsibility – because they want us to see the world as so unlivable that we consent to its destruction. They want us to want to die. We must not be numb.'

It's a sweeping and maudlin declaration. I am in such a mood because at the time I am gazing out onto the Scottish Highlands. It is the summer of 2019, and I am on a long train ride north to Mallaig, and lush greenery flicks by me apace. And so when I read the book and look out onto this, tears do fill my eyes.

*

My name, Eda, is drawn from a common Turkish prayer, which asks Allah for healing for the sick, succour for the distressed, and repayment for the indebted. That last part, relief from or repayment of debt, is what Eda means. Although others have found it a little humorous when I have explained it to them in the past – 'Your name is more, well, financial than I expected' – I appreciate its grounding in the material.

I don't believe in prayer. I do believe in politics. In reality, most of us don't get pulled out of the mud, no matter how hard we wish or work. Most of us lose games of luck and games of skill: for there to be a winner, most of us have to be losers. Most of us don't get plucked up out of the shit. Most of us don't get discovered and don't win some prize and we don't get granted exemptions from everyday indignities. Most of us will not be saved nor save ourselves. What I believe is that we have to alter the conditions of everyday existence, so that there's nothing that we need to be saved from. This requires me to resist fatalism where I can, especially the ways that I see it creeping into my leftism of late. I have chanted *no justice, no peace,* many, many times, but for a long time not realising it did not mean *there is no justice and there is no peace,* but rather that *if there is no justice, there will be no peace:* something much less static, less permanent, and more at hand, more immanent.

When Tex asks me if I practise Islam, I say that I try to enact Alevi principles in substance. At least, I donate 3 per cent of my income to local causes: a woman's shelter in Parramatta, strike funds for workers in Western Sydney, to refugee services, and to Indigenous communities. Less practically, perhaps, I have saved to my computer an image from an Alevi organisation based in Turkey, which uses as its logo the sword of Ali transposed onto a sickle. I am about to have it tattooed, in part inspired by a fellow leftie colleague of mine who has a large tattoo down his arm emblazoned with the phrase BREAD AND ROSES. James Oppenheim, who composed the poem which the union song is based off of, writes,

> As we go marching, marching, in the beauty of the day
> A million darkened kitchens, a thousand mill lofts gray
> Are touched with all the radiance that a sudden sun
>   discloses
> For the people hear us singing, bread and roses, bread and
>   roses.

*

For a very long time I didn't notice that I didn't notice colours. Fellow havers of complex trauma or depression may relate. I didn't make plans for the future. I lived as small a life as possible so that it didn't matter if it ended. And if the world ended, I thought, it would likewise be no great loss. Then I took enough MDMA – sitting alone in my bed for hours at a time, listening to Turkish music and thinking about my family until it didn't feel bad anymore – and sat through enough therapy that one day I was walking down Croydon Street, heading to Petersham Park, and I noticed that jacaranda trees are fantastically purple, and the dead lorikeet that I saw on the road, while dead, was fucking green and its splattered guts were really very red.

When it comes to blasting huge doses of serotonin into my brain, a better, or more affordable, alternative to MDMA, I have discovered, is art. My day job is not an exciting one, nor is it artsy. Mostly, I am a glorified Googler or Microsoft Excel user. I make graphs. I download journal articles. During these tasks, though, I listen to poetry set to music – revolutionary poetry, to be specific, as this is the surest, most romantic way to vivify me. They deal in dirt: are concerned, fundamentally, with the material. I listen to 'Popular Wobbly', a union anthem, and 'Bella Ciao', a partisan anthem, in various languages, and I cry for some reason when I think about the fact that both songs in their lyrics feature a persona who expresses a preoccupation with what will happen to their bodily remains after they die: one asks, after death, if roses will grow atop his body, and the other asks, plaintively, to be buried in the mountains after they go, in the shade of a flower. I decide I want to be buried in a free Turkey, where solculuk – leftism – is revitalised and lives on. When I listen I feel a rush, like I swear I am going to ascend. Like I am going to arrest the flow of fortune and snap the little wheel in two, and I am going to conquer for my parents everything that conquered them. We're going to figure out a way to win. I am going to go back to a free Turkey, wearing my metal detector across my chest like a Ghostbuster. Fuck you! We're all gonna get what we deserve.

These are silly thoughts: brief moments during which I have fallen out of my three-to-seven safe zone of emotional regulation, turned down the elevator jazz and blasted violent rock. But they help me cope.

Western Medicine

I want to go home. Under normal circumstances I might refuse to admit that Milperra, in Sydney's south-west, is in fact far from my home. But the sun has set and I am walking and walking, and it's not the middle of nowhere, but it is an hour and a half away from my place, and I want to go home.

Western Sydney University Bankstown is larger than my campus in Camperdown. I am a postgraduate student at the University of Sydney, but am at WSU for a workshop. Here, the buildings are squat rather than built upwards. The car parks – there are multiple, no *Mad Max*–style competition for parking – are nearly empty, regular classes having long ago finished for the day. I find the availability of space here soothing. My undergraduate days, also at the University of Sydney, had been spent folding myself every morning into the train that left Blacktown at 8.06 am, defending with my elbows the small segment of a pole I managed to secure myself to hold on to, and then wending through the dense CBD to make it to class on time. This feels more breathable. More than that, I feel less racially marked out here, less pressure to disguise what a university professor had once described, before we stepped into a tutorial, as *my accent. Where are you from?* I had made it awkward by answering, *Nowhere, well, from here, I was born here, in Sydney.* I should have answered Western Sydney. What he had detected was my woggish dialect, which is suggestive of my class and that I was raised by immigrants. These are all chimeras of belonging and not-belonging.

I accidentally kick and loosen a paver walking in the dark. I mumble, *Oops, sorry, WSU,* and it earns me an odd look from the woman next to me who I am trying to make small talk with. A little younger than me, she has just finished facilitating the meeting I attended. She is the reason I want to go home. Projecting the air of being a Mean Girl, she is an exemplar of the sub-genre of human that I generally fear, given that I grew up as a chubby, highly bullyable nerd. Her rage is barely concealed. You can see it in the way she has spent the evening critiquing the work of others, implying or openly stating that they are inadequate. I understand these types of people, have learned how to navigate around them, and contort pleasingly to appease them. It doesn't stop me from thinking she's an arsehole, but I have rationalised it as a sort of community service: it must give her gratification that she is otherwise lacking. Besides, I need a lift. There's not much I won't do, won't tolerate, if I get to go home at the end.

(To give an extreme example of my tolerance, last year I shared an Uber with three men that my friends and I met at a Mardi Gras party. We crossed paths at The Bearded Tit in

Redfern, all of them garbed in mesh and rainbow and glitter. I had accepted the lift because the guys' place in Stanmore was around the corner from mine in Petersham, and I planned to turn tail and walk home as soon as we stepped out of the vehicle. But they separated us, parcelling one girl into a different ride, and she, more polite or less shrewd than me, made the mistake of stepping into their house before we arrived. I spent the next two hours exfiltrating the three of us from their home, me containing a rising anger that they had duped us into thinking they were not in fact just like every other predatory heterosexual cis man. I made this realisation as they immediately started pouring generous drinks into our glasses, replenishing them quickly, making increasingly coercive demands that we join them, nude, in their hot tub; that we take some of the coke or ketamine they were offering; that we stay over, despite repeating the hollow adage that we were *welcome to leave at any time*. Attempts I made to move towards the door were blocked, each of us assigned our own lecherous man. I remember the way one of the men's faces hovered near mine, drifting towards me and then back, towards me and then back, his hair sweaty and his shirt half-open, while I projected insouciance. When we finally made it out, we walked arm in arm, cackling with relief, the three of us, back to my place.)

The air is cold so I jam my hands in my coat pockets and make another attempt at polite conversation, asking if I had overheard correctly that the Mean Girl lived in Marayong. The Mean Girl asks where I grew up, and I say, 'Blacktown, just near you.' And then she queries why, if that's true, I'm going to take the train from Bankstown to Strathfield.

'Oh, I moved, actually,' I say, 'when I was nineteen. I live in Strathfield with my partner.'

She hums, and we drop back even further behind the two women whose car we are heading towards. Looking ahead, she asks, 'So did you leave Blacktown because you were ashamed?'

I overestimate the ability of my next response to move her, assuming it will have some chastening effect, like in movies when one party makes some statement about someone's mother and the other party responds, *my mother is dead,* and the other person has to backtrack and apologise.

'No,' I say. 'I moved out of an abusive home, actually.'

The disclosure doesn't elicit the response I had hoped for, which I hoped to take as evidence that I had misinterpreted this person's character, and that she was in fact kind underneath it all. Instead, all she does is hum again, and ask, 'So, does your partner abuse you too?'

I think of that line from *Pride and Prejudice,* wish I could say it: 'You have insulted me in every possible way, and can now have nothing further to say.' But she is not Lady Catherine de Bourg, and I am not clever or handsome like Elizabeth Bennet. Instead, I trail along, hop in the car, even deliver this woman a parting hug at the train station. I go home to my mid-sized apartment in Strathfield, and then, the following year, I move even further east.

*

I think of this exchange often, even though it happened four years ago. It's part of an emergent pattern I have observed in the way that we are encouraged to talk and think about Western Sydney. Only last month a friend of mine received an email telling her she *wasn't really from Western Sydney* by a fellow member of the arts community. He felt she was claiming an identity that did not belong to her, by professing to be from the area, having only lived in Parramatta for two decades, but not during her formative years. If twenty years is not enough, what the hell does it mean to be *from Western Sydney*?

I am loath to think of it as a place with a fixed geography. It's not as sexy to say, but it would be more appropriate to call it a constellation of social meanings stitched together and imputed on an ever-warping set of geographies, with Western Sydney emerging as whatever the centre discards as its periphery. In 1993, the suburb I now live in, Petersham, was considered part of the western suburbs, as were Hurlstone Park and Ashfield. Just as these regions were gentrified prior to my birth, I am now witnessing during my lifetime the gentrification of Harris Park, a suburb next to Parramatta, which I only ever knew as Western Sydney, but which is on the cusp of being reclassified as part of the Inner West. The suburb recently broke into domain.com.au's top 65 for liveability, dragged down only by negative perceptions regarding its crime rates. As Shire-dwellers bleed outwards and southern Sydneysiders hop and skip left into suburbs like Riverwood, Bankstown has, after recent council mergers, been redubbed as Canterbury–Bankstown, and tersely taken on the mantle of belonging to the 'inner city', which does not feel right to many. Why not?

The answer is not so much that different people live in these different places, but rather that these places live in these people. In Bidwill, a Western Sydney suburb in the local government area of my birth, Blacktown, the median lifespan is sixty-nine years. In Cherrybrook, in Sydney's Hills District, where Justin grew up, the median lifespan is eighty-eight years. I know, from experience, that the drive between these two places is only about half an hour, but they do not feel the same. Borders are not, therefore, wholly arbitrary. Although they do not reflect fixed, essential realities, they do shape these realities. We have learned this most potently of late via the designation of some local government areas of Sydney as 'LGAs of concern' (LOC) during the 2021 NSW COVID outbreak. Critics note that this category has created two Sydneys, one where the LOC name carries with it far more restrictive lockdown measures, such as curfews, and has justified the rapid widening of punitive policing in these areas. What is Western Sydney emerges from this differential process: on the same day in September of 2021, a funeral where Muslim attendees remain in their cars to sit silent vigil and grieve is broken up by cops and results in arrests in Lidcome, while I walk to Petersham Park and watch at least one hundred people congregate in the grandstand, blasting music and necking bottles of beer.

*

My father – whose skin is leathery and who has lost every one of his top teeth from lack of care, who drives a twenty-four-year-old manual ute he has to urge up hills through the power of wishing, who still lays bricks at sixty-four, who's down from forty cigarettes a day to twenty because they're so expensive – complains. When he picks me up for my visits, we drive from Blacktown train station to my parents' home, and he goes over the same lines. 'So much more housing.' 'One-bedroom flats selling for one million, can you believe it?' 'I worked in Little Bay in 2001 for a little while. The government decided to make house prices high so they forced out all the Aboriginal people. You know where they put them now? Auburn, in high rises. They used to live by the water.' 'Can you believe our house would sell for 2 million now?' On this last one he takes his eyes off the road, turns to me, gives me a rare open-mouthed smile. It does not last long, because he soon has to shift gears to go up an incline, which requires all his attention and our joint prayers.

My brother-in-law works in Penrith. The warehouse that neighbours his has been empty since February, the previous tenant having died by suicide. In summer, he receives text messages on 45-plus-degree days, advising him to stay cool and indoors, neither of which is possible unless he travels to the nearby Westfield shopping centre. During the 2019 bushfire season, the air quality in the western suburbs was routinely almost twice as bad as in the inner city; my father worked outdoors the whole time. While we were still together, Justin used to plan our future. We discussed that it was not in my interests to inherit my family's Blacktown home, if that were even an option – the area, my area, would be almost uninhabitable in summer by the year 2030. 'So we'll just move to Cherrybrook,' he'd conclude, satisfied.

When I was eighteen I was struggling to obtain a part-time job, couldn't even break into hospitality or retail. I commiserated with Gülin, twenty-one years my elder, inside her Zetland apartment, surrounded by her terrifying topengs and decorative swords. She had at one time earned six-figure *fuck you* money, which she used to buy this home, and she gave me a bit of advice that helped her when she was job-seeking in the nineties.

'Put down my address on your CV,' she said. 'You know, because sometimes people can have a negative idea of Blacktown.' Because I grimaced, she continued, 'It might seem unfair, but it's not far off. For example, I dated this one guy when I was in uni and still living at home. White guy, from the Northern Beaches. Footballer. Tall. He rode the train back with me once as a favour because it was late, and he said even he was afraid to be out there.'

I had rolled my eyes at my abla, and tried to argue that it was the other person's problem if they had an issue with where I lived. But I had changed the address on my CV, and got a job quickly.

Correlation does not equal causation. But these experiences do feel interlaced. They have led me to believe, stridently, that 'being from Western Sydney' is not a social identity. That is, it has little to do with culture – driving a certain car, speaking a certain way, eating a kebab like *this* and not like *this*. This line of thinking intersects heavily with the bourgeois belief that class is a socio-cultural category, and not a material one. It is easy to fake, to roleplay being from Western Sydney if being from Western Sydney means to affect certain speech, aesthetics or taste. But I don't really care about this, and find splitting hairs over who claims to be originally from what part of this continent, all of which is stolen land, a little ridiculous. What I care about is that these class-as-culture arguments pull attention away from class as a material relation, and draw the focus towards eliminating classism instead. I do not agree that the way to uplift people from Western Sydney is to start by eliminating shame and fostering pride in and tolerance of our differences, although I do not dispute that this is important. What is more important is this: to be from Western Sydney, in its essence, is to experience, on a day-to-day basis, the materiality of living. Streets, which are less shaded, more poorly lit, and subject to less urban forest cover. Schools, which receive less funding, upkeep, and even less air-conditioning. Roads, whose lanes are narrower, more pot-holed and more unsafe – you can see and feel the gradient of the asphalt change underneath your wheels if you drive far enough down the M4. Hospitals, which perform worse across several measures. In fact, rankings regularly suggest that five out of the bottom six hospitals in NSW are located in Western Sydney. Trains, which are older, fewer, later, less secure and more crowded. Buildings, where asbestos lurks, and where housing is more high-density and each dwelling has higher the average number of occupants. Auburn, in the Cumberland LGA, an LOC, has the highest rate of people living in 'extremely overcrowded' housing in Sydney, which contributed directly to high rates of COVID transmission during the 2021 outbreak. As the editors of the journal *Infrastructural Inequalities* wrote, 'Infrastructural systems distribute resources, capacities, and harms in differentiated and unjust ways.' To speak of infrastructure may not be hot, but it determines the sexy, sexy lived experiences that result: they are the conditions of possibility for the latter. That some think Blacktown is dangerous, or that I think it is not, for example, is a moot point, only up until the moment where the social meanings ascribed to a place butt up against the material, creating real-world impacts, for example, my employability. Shame, therefore, has little to do with it, and whether I identify as *from here* has little to do with it. It doesn't matter whether I do or do not claim Western Sydney. Western Sydney has claimed me.

*

I was born in the bathroom of Blacktown Hospital. This was the result of my mother going into labour on the toilet, having arrived at the hospital weeks overdue and ready to be induced. I have always joked that this set the tone for what was to come. Every time I see a sign that reads 'female toilet', I think to myself, *that's me!*

The next time I ended up at Blacktown Hospital was also due to cursed sex. Not that all sex is cursed, but the sex that occasioned my birth and the sex that occasioned my hospitalisation certainly were. The latter sex was that which I was having with Justin when I was eighteen, and which gave me a urinary tract infection for which I was prescribed antibiotics. About twelve hours after I took the last tablet, I remember sitting at Hog's Breath Café on the rooftop floor of Blacktown Westpoint with my family, eating steaks and curly fries. As the evening drew to a close my hands began to itch, and under the dim light I noticed that my palms, which clutched a lemon, lime and bitters, were covered in red splotches. By the end of dessert, hives had ascended my arms. Rashes spread across my chest and made their way up my legs overnight, and the following evening my hands were so swollen I couldn't bend my fingers at any of the joints. To gain some relief from the itching I slept with two sandwich bags filled with ice cubes clasped loosely in my fat pink palms.

I rushed to the medical centre the following morning. Blacktown's Main Street is lined with medical centres, many of them owned by the same Turkish doctor. It goes like this: fruit and veg grocer that sells eight types of mango by the box. African hairdresser or Indian clothing boutique. Next a pharmacy, then a kebab shop. Every ten storefronts a medical centre. The doctor quickly, but incorrectly, surmised I had contracted a virus not unlike chickenpox.

'Have you been around children lately?' he asked, waiting for me to bashfully pull up my pants after I, unsolicited, had insisted on showing him the hives that had now spread to my legs, and which he did not inspect.

At the time I was volunteering at a not-for-profit providing literacy and numeracy tutoring to the over 5,600 Sudanese Australians in New South Wales, many of them recently settled here as refugees, and 40 per cent of whom live in Blacktown. I had nodded. He issued me with a low dose of prednisone and I left. The next day my blood pressure fell so low, from an undiagnosed allergic reaction to amoxycillin, that I passed out on the stairs, having made it to the bottom floor of my family's Blacktown rental before I collapsed, lucky I hadn't broken my neck.

Through the course of the next five hours at Blacktown Hospital's emergency room, I eventually got access to a drip bag of antihistamines. The staff did not have a bed for me, so they placed me, in a wheelchair, into a corner, to maximise the efficiency of my lumpy body's use of space. A medical student cannulised me, forgetting to undo the elastic strap she had fixed around my arm, and I watched, unamused, as my arm tracked a gradient from pink to purple, as I meekly tried to flag down any member of staff, like a patron at a busy restaurant, to ask if I was allowed to take it off. I still have a crooked toe in a right foot, resulting from an injury sustained in 2010 – a fracture and dislocation that was not relocated. The toe sticks out of my shoes and it's easy to laugh about.

In 2020, over 100 nurses and midwives staged a walkout of Blacktown Hospital in response to the rate of neonatal deaths that occurred there, not replicated in any other hospital in New South Wales: six in two years, the result of inadequate staffing and burnout among overworked midwives and doctors. Not only does the hospital service a large population of child-rearing age, but the births themselves are more likely to be complex, given underlying health conditions among the population.

The next time I break some part of my foot – the heel this time, which I shatter in 2020 – I go to the Royal Prince Alfred Hospital in Camperdown, which attracts over $300 million worth of funding per year more than Blacktown Hospital. Justin comes with me, deposits me into a wheelchair that a nurse trundles out, and then goes off to park my car. Before he can return, I am through the waiting room and having an x-ray taken. Although the injury presents as a severe sprain, a doctor takes a careful enough look at my imaging to notice that I do indeed have a fracture – multiple, in fact – that are notorious for going undetected if insufficient attention is paid. Studies show that when this is not picked up, the type of injury that I sustained lingers for up to six months longer than when the appropriate diagnosis is made at the right time. These facts are not sexy, and nor is my right foot. Not only does the toe stick out, but I now have what I describe to my friends as a 'new bone'. I love to peel off my sock, and show off how the healing and re-modelling process that has taken place in my mid-foot has caused one of the bones there to move into a new location, now protruding; these small things, silly things, really, marking the past of my body.

*

When I was seven my mother returned to Turkey to tend to my grandmother, who was wasting away, dying of Hepatitis C, in a public hospital in İzmir. When blood supplies ran low at this hospital, it was Gülin's job to buy some more from the nearby blood bank, carting the bags back to the hospital by taxi. Gülin was also the first on site after my grandmother was hospitalised in 2000. My grandmother had thrown up blood all over her apartment in Üçkuyular while dragging herself bodily through the apartment, trying to make it from the bedroom to the phone. Gülin had taken the first flight from Amsterdam, where she had been working, to İzmir, and tasked herself with cleaning up the carnage in the flat. Blood had soaked the floor, and splattered up and down the walls, and she had diligently mopped it up, without protection, lucky not to contract the virus herself.

Left with the care of myself and my eleven-year-old sister, my father warehoused us at OOSH in the afternoons, returning from work in Little Bay at dusk, exhausted from a day of hard labour, and drove us to the nearby Macca's to set us up with an easy meal. By the time my mother returned from burying her mother three months later, she says the two of us were unrecognisable from weight gain. Ten to twenty per cent of Mount Druitt and Blacktown residents live within a kilometre of a takeaway, but do not have access to a supermarket in the same distance. People living in Western Sydney are one-and-a-half times more likely to develop diabetes than in other parts of Sydney, and two times more likely to die of heart disease. We can't help it that we're so sweet – or that our pancreases are in arrears.

When depression hit at eleven, all I did was cry, unable to stop until three or four hours had passed and I was left sobbing without being able to produce tears. The word 'FAT', that I would write on my belly in kiddie metallic texta, upside down, was hard to conceal. My mother caught a glimpse of this marking one day, asking me to hold up my t-shirt to show her and my sister, both of whom were angry and insisted that I wash it off. A friend of mine, on the other hand, would throw up. Every weekend her mother would follow her to the public toilet after meals at Parramatta food court in order to eavesdrop on her vomiting, my friend denying that anything had happened and her mother hysterical and disbelieving. This friend explains that she also began to pull out her hair, strand by strand, and by the time she was fourteen she was her ideal weight, and her scalp was bald in places. Neither of us has ever been treated for an eating disorder, a mental illness that is notoriously stereotyped as uniquely middle-class, white, female, and therefore frivolous. When I have visited GPs in my adult life, in Blacktown, expressing concern about my body, I have always been more worried about my relationship with it than what's happening to it. The least engaged of these doctors have usually responded to my requests for bloodwork and other tests by sashaying their way down the following checklist: Do you drink? Do you smoke? Are you pregnant? Are you *sure* you're not pregnant? Do you understand what junk food is, which you must be eating a lot of, or do you need to see a dietitian? I can't help but see race and class in these lines of questioning, a belief that it is my ignorance or my intentional disregard for my health and propriety that has caused my body to malfunction.

It takes me several years to be diagnosed with polycystic ovary syndrome and Hashimoto's disease – only after I make my regular GP the one at the University of Sydney, where

I am named in my file as a member of staff, and never have to explain that I understand the basics of contraception and nutrition. My doctor orders me the tests I need without my having to beg for them, and the resulting diagnoses yield me a real explanation for my sudden physical symptoms. When I start treating them, I finally feel like I have restored control over my body, control I had lost for at least five years, so busy was I trying to do the homework I was assigned by other doctors seen in the past, before I was middle-class, learning the difference between animal, vegetable, mineral and fucking foetus.

*

Months after my mother is diagnosed, she continues to repeat the refrain that the blackness in her soul made its way into her bones. Gülin had texted her something along these lines – içinin siyahı kemiklerine geçmiş – after my mother had insisted on sending my sister an image of her discoloured joints, made brittle by a build-up of homogentisic acid. The joint in question had been freshly removed from her knee and slapped onto a surgical surface, photographed by a startled surgeon who had no idea what he was looking at. My mother shows the photograph to most people that she meets – an impulse, to be witnessed in her suffering, that I understand.

'Don't text her,' I had warned. 'She's going to say something to upset you.'

But my mother had. I wonder if her preoccupation with blackness represents a later-in-life realisation that she has hurt and harmed us, and whether she feels some guilt. Before the diagnosis in 2018, she had blamed me for her ailing back and joint pain; her reasons were sound enough that I didn't press it. I was in a pram during the accident. So I am not a reliable witness.

When I was twelve, treading water in the indoor pool of Blacktown Aquatic Centre, I asked if I could see a psychologist for my sadness. I remember that my mother peeled off her goggles, which had fogged from her instant tears.

'How did I fail you as a parent?' she asked.

I said, 'You didn't.'

'What do you need a psychologist for? You haven't seen the things I've seen. Sen benim gördüklerimi bir bilsen.'

She launched into an explanation of how she fell down the stairs of Marayong Public School while pushing me in the pram, and irreversibly injured her spine. I'd just learnt the phrase 'non sequitur' but didn't know the word for it in Turkish, so instead I spat out chlorinated piss-water and pulled myself up onto the edge.

'How is that relevant?'

'My life would be so much better if you hadn't been in that pram, çocuğum. You have your health. If anyone should be unhappy, it's me.'

'We can both be unhappy,' I said. And so it was.

It turns out, however, that I am not the reason she has experienced debilitating joint pain since she was thirty, not the reason her own father used to get beaten as a young man during his military service because his knees were so arthritic he could not kneel on command. Now, my mother blames the doctors who failed to diagnose her sooner, although I insist it might not have made a difference. There is no cure for alkaptonuria.

'I knew something was wrong with my body,' she repeats. 'I knew it. Ama hiç kimse beni dinlemedi. Bana inanmadılar. Göçmen olduğum için'.

I understand her relentless questing a little better after the diagnosis, can see why most weekends with her growing up were spent being carted from one doctor to another. I understand, a little better now, why I have been interpreting test results and medical reports from specialists since I was a child, my mother growing agitated and insistent that I must understand the medical terminology because I speak English, and that the times I do not understand I am simply being defiant or do not care enough about her to help. At some point I gave up remarking that I had no medical training. Instead, I simply learned. I can recite easily all the medication she takes, for example, fill out forms for her by rote, and have easily stepped into the role of her medical advocate now. I am happy to do this, if it means the quality of her life improves.

But I worry that her malaise might not have the name she thinks it does. I remember all the times my mother and I squabbled about the same subject, as soon as I turned eighteen, me arguing that she could divorce him, leave and go back, go home, please, don't stay on my account. *I'll even pay the airfare,* I offered. And each time she would conclude, *I can't go back. I'm too sick to fly.* And each time, I would simply remark back, *You* are *sick.*

I still cannot differentiate between which illnesses are real and imagined. She has been bedridden since I was a child, abstractly sick. I receive daily updates about her illnesses – coronary artery disease, kidney failure, fatty liver disease, heel spurs, rheumatoid arthritis, pinched nerves, a stomach ulcer, a hernia, ocular hypertension, throat cancer, stomach cancer, swine flu, COVID. When I was younger, all of her communiques about her health concluded with *come visit your mother*, and each felt like the time she was actually going to be terminal. Sometimes I have believed it so thoroughly I have told friends she is dying, and then I have had to reassess, in the cold light of day, what had made me believe that, after I visit and confirm she is just as she ever was. Now that I am older and less likely to fall for this – or perhaps I am more heartless – she instead sends me instructions, names of people to call, requests to make, complaints to lodge. I think she deserves this, even if I feel manipulated. Rather, I think that even if she were a stranger to me, even a stranger would deserve someone who could clear away for them racism and xenophobia and sexism.

I try to insist to her that the belated diagnosis is nobody's fault – although she has me telephone former doctors and ask them to pull records, look through historical medical imaging CDs, searching for proof that the evidence was there all along but overlooked – if only so that she lets go of her anger. I wonder if I also deserve a share in that rage. I've had things taken from me too: the answer to the question of what sort of parent she might have been without her disease, for example. That depends on determining the exact limits of the causal power of chronic pain, a counter-factual I could fill with whatever content I wanted. Any fantasy.

We should all be judged by the person we are when we are not in pain – it's easy to be polite, kind, respectable in these moments. But not even pain is distributed equitably. It too intensifies or lessens based on social factors, and is spread unevenly through the populace. In the United States, for example, black people are less likely to be prescribed opioid pain relievers, despite being less likely to misuse them. In Australia in 2014, a twenty-two-year-old Aboriginal woman, Ms Dhu, lay dying in police custody, complaining of excruciating chest pain caused by sepsis and pneumonia. During her time in custody, she was taken to a hospital twice, both times being deemed dishonest about her pain level and discharged with inadequate care, on her latter visit only with a few paracetamol. She died while a police constable stood over her insisting that she was faking.

I want to take away my mother's pain. I make it my mission, briefly, in 2020, deciding that cannabidiol is a superior natural alternative to opioids, which are addictive and known to grow ineffective with long-term use. It takes months to access a prescription for CBD oil in Australia, so I am gifted some pot brownies from a friend as a first measure. He drives me with them from Parramatta to my mother's home in Blacktown, and I am so grateful for the gesture I feel like crying. I want to know if they will change who she is, so I coax her into consuming half of one right away. The brownie gives her a panic attack – felling good for a moment, she goes on to eat the whole thing, a rookie error from us both – and for the rest of the night we sit on the couch doing breathing exercises, which I myself have become the expert at from having regular panic attacks for over fifteen years. We breathe for five, hold for five, exhale for five. I ask my mother to name the colour of the couch, to tell me her name, to tell me my name, to describe what she's wearing, to list off our birthdays, until she calms down. Then we go into the backyard so she can inhale the crisp night air, and I lay a blanket over her when she gets cold, and she looks at me, and she says, 'Eda, if I die tonight –'

'You're not going to die,' I sigh. God, I'm tired.

'*If* I die,' she insists, then slants a look at me, 'don't blame yourself too much, okay?'

*

My mother's brother died when he was twenty-one and my mother was seventeen. He had colon cancer that had spread so far before it was misdiagnosed that a tumour large enough to protrude from his anus had been operated on as if it were a prolapsed haemorrhoid. By this time the cancer had spread to his brain. My mother's father never sought treatment for his hypertension, insisting doctors had killed his son. He died from a heart attack with a cigarette still burning in his mouth.

I didn't get to say goodbye, said my mother, after the family back in Turkey finally admitted it. She had asked to speak with him, over the phone, for two months, and they stonewalled for worry she would squander having shed her qualifications in Turkey to become a cleaner in Australia and pack up and return.

'Not even I said goodbye,' said my grandmother.

*

Because I am short-sighted, and start becoming that way from a very young age, I visit an optometrist every year for an eye-check starting at age six. I dread these appointments, because my vision, inevitably, always grows worse, and it is always my fault. My mother sometimes cries, sometimes yells: 'Eda, what are you doing to yourself? Kendine ne yapıyorsun? Kör edeceksin kendini.'

One year, my prescription doubles, and this is the year my mother bans me from reading more than one page of a book a day, to preserve my eyesight. It cements a belief that I will have, in my lifespan, a finite number of words or pages I can read before I use up all my vision. I hide a copy of *Harry Potter and the Goblet of Fire* in my room, and I sneak extra pages.

Pekmez turns my stomach. All it is is grape molasses, but it is heralded as a medicinal superfood by some Turks. My mother gets into the habit of forcing a tablespoon of it down my throat every morning, almost like a dog having my mouth clamped shut until I swallow. Its health benefits are myriad, according to my mother. All I know is it turns my shit black. When I remark on this fact casually, my mother concludes that I have a gastrointestinal bleed, and I have to shit the pekmez shit into a bucket for several days until the stool test clears me. Pekmez giveth and pekmez taketh away.

I have a brief fainting spell when I am twelve – I pass out for five to ten seconds after I stand up too quickly, barely fall down. My mother thinks I have epilepsy. We go to Westmead

Hospital for an EEG: they flash lights in my face, while I wait to have a seizure. They tape electrodes to my face and ask me to sleep, but it is daytime so I can only achieve something resembling an uncomfortable nap. I don't have epilepsy.

For several months in primary school, I am not allowed to run laps on the oval. When I make to do so, unaware that my mother has asked that I be exempted from sports due to my asthma – which Tex does not believe I ever had, given I cannot recall a single time in my life I had an asthma attack – the teacher calls me back with a frantic shout. 'Not you, Eda,' she says. In response to my confusion: 'You're sick.'

My spine isn't straight. I don't know how my mother figures it out; I am old enough that she has not seen me topless for years. We visit the GP, who asks me to take my shirt off, including my bra, and she examines me, passing her hands down my back, trailing the shape of my spine. I don't want to take all my clothes off with my mother in the room, but my mother promises she will cover her eyes, makes a show of holding her hands up to her face. When we step out of the office, she remarks that she had taken a peek after all, when I was bending down and had averted my gaze, and that my breasts were much larger than she expected. I have mild scoliosis, which I have to inform my fellow students of at school, when they ask why I have been assigned a special locker to store my books. 'What's wrong with you that you got that?' one asks.

One night, when I am a child, I dart from the bedroom that my sister and I share into my mother's bedroom. I whisper until she wakes up, and I tell her that I can't stop pissing – I have woken up several times that night to go, feeling a burning surge, but not much comes out. My mother rolls over, her voice rough with sleep and anger, at me, and says, 'Good. That's what happens. Keep holding it in.' I don't realise she is being sarcastic, and I take this as sincerely meant advice. I hold it in. Despite this, I get better. When she recalls the interaction a few days later, and inquires as to my health, I comment, pleased, that her advice had helped. She hits me with the switch we kept in the bathroom, which usually we kids held out in front of us, while on the toilet, like Gandalf the Great taking a shit. It helped us with the strain, somehow. It was also the cane reserved for hitting us when we didn't piss enough times a day. This mystical cane that controlled our bodily fluids. Five years later, when I was ten, I found myself timing my trips to the bathroom to the half hour for a full month. I determined that if I did not piss twice an hour I would die. I hadn't made the connection until I. Wrote. This. Sentence.

*

There is something wrong with me. At times I am unshakeably convinced of this fact. I have undergone enough therapy in my life to know that I have what is called a defectiveness schema, or perhaps complex PTSD: in either case, I have come away from a few of my life experiences believing that I am not like anybody else. Even if I am not worse, I am different, marked out to be different. If something bad hasn't yet happened to me, it will. This fear centralises on my body, which I believe is feeble, ill. Sometimes I take measures to make it so: to not feed it, or feed it too much, or smoke darts, or decide that exercise is for everybody else and I am one of those people who must hide their body away, lest anyone realise that there is something deeply, deeply wrong with me.

I finally start discussing health anxiety in therapy in 2021, having been unwilling to name it for what it was for years prior, so convinced was I that I was indeed ill rather than imagining myself ill. The lines between these two things are very flimsy, but there are two incidents that convinced me to seek help.

The first occurs when my heel is still shattered, and it leads to my second visit to the Royal Prince Alfred Hospital emergency department – my friends and I start joking that I am treating it like a drive-through, there almost every day. I am having a panic attack. I have just taken my broken foot out of its bandage for the first time in about ten days, and noticed the large bruise running down the side. Justin's mother is over at our house when she notices it, and she remarks passively that it looks fresh, like something new has gone wrong. I decide, spontaneously, that what I must have is compartment syndrome, because, more than any other injury complication, it has the potential to be fatal, and of course I am dying. My partner dutifully drives us to the ER, reassuring me the whole time that it's better to be safe than sorry. On the way, he calls one of his friends, a recent medical graduate.

'You may as well go if you like,' she remarks, and with my shaky voice I say thanks and leg it to the entrance.

We repeat the process of wheeling me into the waiting area, like the exact erotic opposite of a magician's assistant: *ta-da!* I am ill. A trainee nurse, who remarks to a colleague that she has just arrived here from Blacktown Hospital, takes my temperature and my vitals. My blood pressure and heart rate are high, and I'm even running a fever.

'I think I might just be stressed,' I remark, the realisation dawning, as I stare, in a dissociated state, at the bright lights on the ceiling, until a doctor arrives. He glances at my foot, concludes that bruising is a natural and normal consequence of falling down, and sends me home. This is the first time I ever go to the ER for a panic attack, and I decide I have to work on making it my last.

A few months later, my foot is healed and I am driving again, regularly. I drive the thirty-something kilometres to Max Webber Library in Blacktown every Monday in order to volunteer with an organisation that tutors children with low literacy levels. The drive back is always stressful, because I make it at 5 pm. Some weeks, I sit in the lane waiting to turn onto West Street, metres from my house, for up to half an hour. Doing so makes me, at random, start quaking like a chihuahua one day, and after that I become obsessively fearful that I am going to need to piss while driving and won't be able to. I convince myself it is a UTI, again, and even take a full course of antibiotics. I am in excruciating, completely psychosomatic pain, for several nights. When my GP calls to inform me that my urine test has turned up no evidence that I have an infection, I summarily delete the voicemail and realise that I am going crazy, which might be a good thing to nip in the bud.

When we discuss health anxiety in therapy, my psychologist asks me to start at my head and work my way down my body, identifying which diseases or ailments I have been, at various points, convinced I have.

'Well,' I say. 'Obviously, there was the time I thought I had a brain tumour, so I had a brain CT.' She nods, and, that checked off, I start to trace both my hands down my body, stopping occasionally. 'Um, my greatest fear at the moment is that I will go blind.' It does not help that when I have panic attacks, my vision blurs, and I do see flashing lights, which my optometrist has warned me will be the only sign that my retina is detaching, if it were to happen.

'What about your hearing?' says my psychologist. 'You've never been afraid you'll lose your hearing?'

'Oddly,' I say, 'no. I think that if I had enough control over my brain to decide what part of me I think is broken, then I would have control over this illness in general, wouldn't I?'

Being a little smartarse. She shrugs, and I keep working my way down: to an imagined hernia, ovarian cancer, sexually transmitted diseases, blood clots, endless immaculate pregnancy scares. I forget to list half of them and kick myself later, as if I have failed to prove that I am an unreliable witness of my body. We discuss why I have ended up in this place, and I lament that when I was a child I could not notice anything, regularly missed signs of discomfort. Studies show that those who experience trauma grow numb to their bodies: those with the most severe trauma cannot even recognise themselves in a mirror, or know when someone is, for example, holding onto a body part like their foot.

'I missed so much,' I remark. 'I just kept missing stuff. And I'm afraid one day I'm going to miss something big, so I keep watching myself, telling myself that "this is it, this is the thing". I'm overcompensating for all the times I couldn't notice my body – now I can't stop.'

My psychologist lectures me about how robust I am. It's one of her favoured words: relationships must be robust, communication must be robust, I must be robust.

'Tell me,' she says, 'are you actually physically unhealthier than anyone else in your age group?'

'I'm short-sighted,' I respond, already hearing how much I have missed the question. I try to ham it up. '*Severely* short-sighted,' but it sounds frail even to my ears, which hear perfectly well.

She reminds me I will never lose my eyesight, even if my eyes are a bit shit, except for when I am grey and old. She convinces me I am just as healthy or unhealthy as anyone else. I decide I should probably learn how to inhabit or befriend or even just tolerate my body, so I take up boxing lessons. I stand in Petersham Park twice a week, on the oval, exposed, watched, and I do comical things with my body: I draw imaginary eggs in the air with my arm extended, I punch the air while walking backwards, I get my glasses knocked off my face a couple of times. Once, I even manage a joke, when my glasses have been newly thrown off my face, and landed in a bush, and a man stops me to ask if I know where the bathroom is. I respond, 'The loos are by the pool. I'm not wearing my glasses and even I know that.' He is angry, but I feel proud that I can laugh about my shit eyes. Afterwards, I go home and I take a bath, and the pain is not so bad.

Literacy

Words only get us so far. I only say this because Lacan does. Words fail us, and it is impossible to say the whole truth. Sometimes I am speechless, unsure about how or why I should speak, or convinced I cannot, and turn instead towards silence, dissimulation, deal in omissions. At times even the act of writing operates more like a lid than a container, closing off access to the thing-in-itself I am trying to reach. Like throwing coats on a bed until you can no longer see the bed. I write down a memory and it becomes a story. I render a person and they become a character, one, perhaps, now able to be deconstructed, held up to the light and turned at many angles, searching for the right analysis. A friend of mine teaches creative non-fiction, and she instructs her students to determine what the central inquiry of their work is: what question it is that they are carrying around with them in their gut. Mine is, 'Why is my mother the way that she is, and why am I the way that I am?' They are the same question.

I lean on Lacan, return to Lacan, because it is easier to speak authoritatively by using someone old, dead and French as a mouthpiece. I don't have the strength of my convictions: I have the strength of Jacques Lacan's. I would say Lacan and I are so close he is like a father, but that would be a freebie. Far too easy to read into. You've got to work for it. That's what Lacan taught me.

What is not easy to read into is Lacan. His work forms a key component of the post-structuralist tradition, an intellectual movement with which I have a complex relationship. On one hand, it's high theory: writing on culture and literature that is wordy, at times impenetrable, and so thoroughly abstracted from everyday life that one feels self-conscious consuming it, feels at risk of fulfilling the stereotype of the latte-sipping ivory tower wanker. These kinds of work hinge on symbolism: in it, the world and its people become reduced to abstracted bodies and spaces, and power spoken about in terms of discourse, language and subjectivation, rather than structures, resistance, labour and unions. Post-structuralism refuses to make general diagnoses about who exactly is doing the oppressing and why, which makes it difficult to know where to aim our fire. At times I have found this alienating, gravitating towards Marxism instead, certain that the history of all hitherto existing society is the history of class struggle, or, in other words, that there are structures at play here, namely that one that sees those with wealth take from those without. On the other hand, I spend much of my time reading this work, studying it, teaching it, joying in it. Detractors of post-structuralism criticise its focus on language, and argue that language is not life, and I agree – but language has helped me with the task of living.

Take 'The Function and Field of Speech and Language in Psychoanalysis', a paper we were assigned to read for Literary Theory class in 2015, my fourth year of university, as an example. *Four years for an Arts degree?* I know. Lacan did a medical degree in five, and only after he was deemed too thin to join the military. *A skinny doctor?* My mother would love him. And Lacan loved mothers, of course.

Lacan's work on psychoanalysis was meant to help us interpret texts, because the unconscious is structured like a language – so language is structured like the unconscious? Maybe.

None of us understood but none of us would admit it. We were all a little lost, but wonderfully lost, under the tutelage of Dr Bruce Gardiner. He was the most famous of the professors they threw at you in undergrad, in my opinion; a litmus test of whether one had the chops to survive further study in English lit – and one would think, who *doesn't* have the chops to survive English lit? It's more difficult than you'd think. Admittedly, much of the difficulty that English undergrads faced was a result of contrivance – there is that adage that all French post-structuralists complicated their writing by at least 10 per cent, to convince a French audience they were profound thinkers – but that contrivance happened to be meaningful to me at the time.

Dr Bruce Gardiner padded into class each week, in one of his bright jumpers with a sensible collar peeking out, to slot behind his lectern and survey us from behind these huge retro specs, which rendered his face bug-like. His classes were not unlike sermons, in that each one was used to convince us of ideas we would, under any other circumstances, find both dubious and unnecessarily sexualised. I took to staring cross-eyed at his can of Diet Coke – he consumes exactly one every day, he admitted once, in a rare moment of personal disclosure, and we found it violently cute. He drank from it and replaced it in line with his handwritten lecture notes after every sip, while I typed everything that he said, verbatim, without looking down at my screen, to be processed and understood later.

One day he drew us into a momentary collective psychosis wherein, by the end of the class, its climax, if I may, after he built up to it, at great length, we came away believing that the final lines of A.E. Housman's poem 'The Carpenter's Son' were actually about the narrator ejaculating into the face of a judge:

> Make some day a decent end,
> Shrewder fellows than your friend.
> Fare you well, for ill fare I:
> Live lads, and I will die.

'A murderous masturbation,' he announced. We in-putted the sentence dutifully into our laptops, the *tak-tak* of our typing in concert. I added, confused but thrilled, 'What the fuck?'

In 2013, when the University of Sydney announced its plan to lay off academic staff whose research output did not conform to certain metrics, Bruce Gardiner's name had been tossed around, to be chucked in a bin like a can of Diet Coke. He was the type of academic who had devoted his time to teaching above other pursuits, and thousands and thousands of dull-headed first-years at that. I had had my first exposure to him in my first year of university, in fact, just the year before the proposed axing. There was collective uproar: former students from decades past emerged to defend his contributions, and a petition was circulated which we all signed, because angry university students and petitions go together like wine and cheese. He may have diverted half of his students (away to other studies), but he also diverted (amused, mind-fucked) the remaining half. I perhaps imprinted on Dr Gardiner because of the extent to which I needed such diversion in my first year, to belay my own suicide.

Our Bruce Gardiner did keep his job – and I did not commit suicide, although these two things are only loosely correlated – and continued to make us think so hard we forgot there was ever a thing other than books and words and poetry. We did this thinking in myriad mental positions and in all sorts of locations around campus: in the most opulent of the University of Sydney's Quadrangle Building lecture theatres, for example, with its wooden rows on which we now laid our laptops, splintered and dented by the accumulated presses of heavy pens, its floor-length curtains and its leadlight doors. That day, Bruce Gardiner went in on Christina Rossetti's 'Goblin Market', meditating on the ruthlessness with which he thought the poem withheld its rhymes, frustrated that they were yielded only after delays during which the reader's anticipation for them built and built.

He was describing the practice of orgasm control, of course, and we all knew it this time, because we were fourth years and virgins no longer. Bruce Gardiner argued that Rosetti did this because, quote, 'The character of Laura is caught in a type of – goblin porn addiction, which Lizzie is trying to break her out of. When Lizzie warns Laura to remember Jeannie, she actually does so in order to open Laura's eyes to the ecstasies of self-repression, and show her that masochism eclipses indulgence as a source of pleasure.'

We nodded – hard, but not too hard.

The topic of repression brings us back around to Lacan.

'Lacan tells us that books are symptoms,' said Bruce Gardiner. Someone in the row behind me sneezed. 'They are metaphors. You must read their gaps, what's missing in them, look only toward their accidentals, to see what's really going on.'

Lacan called symptoms *sinthomes,* which is a pretentious Hellenic (which is a pretentious word for Greek) word for symptom. According to Lacan, a symptom is the meaning that the subject cannot access on a conscious level – an outcrop of the unconscious, repressed things externalised by manifesting on the flesh. A sinthome represents the truth, or the unconscious, which can only be deciphered by paying attention to blanks, falsehoods, and censored chapters.

As an example, Lacan says that James Joyce's books were *sinthomes* – things slipped and bubbled out, his works blurted onto the page, releasing some aspect of his psyche in the gaps between deliberation and craft. Reading them for what was present or intended, in fact, closed off one's access to Joyce. Your only inroad was through the gaps, and the lies. Everything else a cover. I was inclined to think James Joyce's intensely scatological love letters to his wife, Nora Barnacle, were more symptomatic of what lay within, so to speak. I was momentarily distracted wondering whether James Joyce did or did not know what a queef was, but held my peace. I could not say these things out loud in these hallowed halls without being a professor. No one cared what I thought. Yet. Or, admittedly, since.

But I enjoyed the stimulation. Enjoyed learning new ways of reading. Enjoyed imbibing Gayatri Spivak and Fredric Jameson and Inga Muscio and Helene Cixous and Theodor Adorno and talking shit in class – speaking about topics which were wonderfully optional, the stakes somehow non-existent but vital at the same time – and rolling out at 5 pm and making the walk down Eastern Avenue while the sky was orange and students lolled about on the lawns and my mind pinged and tumbled around and learned the measure of words like *phenomenology* and *futurity*. The pleasure of inputting my opinions about texts into the form of essays was unparalleled. Criticism is a form of creativity I am attracted to because I have come to see that I am an argumentative person who is frequently convinced that my angle, my take, on a matter, is the right one. This kind of delusional self-belief is not rewarded in many other spheres of social life – so I write essays.

For the course's major assessment, a long essay requiring us to apply a theory of literary criticism to a text of our choosing, I undertook a reading of EM Forster's novel *Maurice*. The least popular of his oeuvre, the book was published after the author's death, intentionally held back for posthumous release because it dealt with queer subject matter. This does not mean it was not distributed widely in typescript among his immediate circle, though: it was read by peers including Stephen Spender, Siegfried Sassoon and even potentially DH Lawrence. Eponymously titled after its protagonist, Maurice Hall, a middle-class man, represses his homosexuality from childhood. At Oxford, he enters into a romantic, but sexless, relationship with a gentry-class man, Clive Durham. Clive insists that the only way for two men to have a relationship is by keeping it purely platonic, and after a sterile relationship with Maurice, turns towards pursuits befitting a squire: marriage and politics. Maurice, due to the breakdown of this relationship, first has sex and then slowly falls in love with Alec Scudder, the working-class under-gamekeeper at Clive's rural estate, Penge. The book concludes, crucially, with a happy ending, as the two men together flee the call of class, living for the rest of their days in idyllic seclusion in nearby greenwood as woodcutters. I had read and reread the book several times since 2010, charmed by its happy ending, after I discovered four EM Forster rare editions clustered on a back shelf of the second-hand bookstore in Castle Hill Mall, which I visited often in my childhood and which has since been torn down. I sat them next to me on the bus home and admired them often – they had pride of place on the bookshelf my father had built me, which I took from rental to rental growing up. These rentals were scattered across Blacktown. My first house was a white fibro, which was demolished when I was ten, and my brickie father undertook to rebuild us our dream home in its place – a built-in bookcase was going to wrap around two walls of my bedroom. My family rented for the next ten years, first a home on Norfolk Street, just down the road from the KFC on Blacktown's main artery, Richmond Road. Our street always smelt of fried chicken, like a fabulous mirage in a food desert. Later, we moved to a home across the road from the first – a quick glance out the window allowed us to see-not-see the construction site that was going to become a house one day, many years later, long after I had moved out and now that none of us can stand to be in the same space together for very long, but at the time obscured by a high metal fence covered in black tarp.

I memorised certain passages from *Maurice* that I liked and typed them up, a ritual I completed for every book I read during my adolescence, like a secular florilegium. 'I get used to being horrible, as you call it, as the poor do their slums. It's only a matter of time. After you've banged about a bit you get used to your particular hole.' That line, spoken by Maurice, the eponymous character, gave me much comfort despite the lack of self-awareness demonstrated by the speaker. Maurice knew shit-all about poverty. So did I. My father was the one who built bookshelves. I put books on them. Only once I was in university did I discover that everyone who mattered hated *Maurice*. Reviewers found the book puerile for daring

to imagine a happy ending for a gay couple in Edwardian
England. They called the two characters' escape into the
greenwood fantastical, an act of wish-fulfillment more akin
to a fairytale. Canny audiences of the book also read the exit
of the characters from society as a symptom of the author's
own repression and self-loathing, given that Forster was not
publicly out as a gay man during his lifetime. To answer this
symptomatic reading of *Maurice* – which sees the novel as
nothing more than an expression of Forster's private queer
angst – and to honour the impact the work had had on
my life, I proposed an alternative angle, another method of
appraising the text that ferreted out the novel's redeeming
features, guided by a desire to prove that those things that
are hard to love can be redeemed by a mode of inquiry that
centres love.

Eve Kosofsky Sedgwick, a queer theorist who I was
first exposed to in Bruce Gardiner's literary theory classes,
outlines a useful distinction between two different modes
of reading, one of which she calls paranoid and the other
reparative. Paranoid reading, she says, stakes a claim to truth
by positing that the only way to know, and to read, a world
replete with loss and pain is to respond with paranoia and
depression, that the only way to interact with awareness of
systemic oppression is to despair. Reparative reading, on
the other hand finds and organises knowledge differently,
responding to it by seeking pleasure and nourishment, as
well as amelioration. Negative readings of *Maurice*'s happy
ending, I argued in my essay, were paranoid, requiring that
we read the book cynically, as if it were the final escapist

death throe of a repressed gay man. I advocated, instead, that we try to view it as a utopic object because of the way it imagines queer love outside of the constraints of class. Forster held back the book during his lifetime, yes, making the choice to dedicate his novel to a 'Happier Year'. Doing so, I argued, allows us to imagine the book as an object sent, as if by time machine, into the future, with all the potentiality and optimism that this represents. Critics have found this decision banal, a sign of the author's disengagement from the present. But I think these kinds of readings mistake cynicism for insight, and in fact introduce errors into the historical record. If these readings of *Maurice* were allowed to prevail, then we might continue to interpret the book as a 'homosexualised *Lady Chatterly's Lover*,' when in fact it is likely the book was read in typescript by DH Lawrence years before he wrote his novel: so is one text really any more banal than the other? These kinds of responses to texts are regularly deemed naïve, pious, complaisant, merely aesthetic or merely reformist. I am not saying that the book is radical per se. But I do think that it is a radical act to read reparatively, guided by a desire to formulate the most generous interpretations possible.

In order to write this essay I read Lacan's *Écrits*. I read it while sealed in my mother's house on a long visit, ensconced in a fleece robe left over from childhood, and hidden during the day in a spare room, willing her not to say anything to me, aware that sometimes her needling became tears became shouting became a domestic and the coppers came around on special occasions, and I hadn't the time for all that, for I had a mission. I had to learn about the Name of the Father. I had to understand that when a child is old enough to apprehend speech, it grasps an important 'no' that the father speaks. This is the 'no' that severs the child's connection to its mother, namely the child's desire for the mother, to be the penis for the mother that the mother lacks. With his 'no', the father clarifies to the child that his penis is the penis that is the mother's penis. This introduction to the incest taboo, a stand-in for cultural norms writ large, marks the child's entry into the Symbolic order (the world of language). Having now departed the Imaginary order, the child loses its previous sense of plenitude, oneness and its inability to tell itself apart from others, all of which had comprised its former access to the Real. Et voilà. What a load of wank, right? Wonderful in its uselessness. Smoke and mirror stages. Theoretically dirty as fuck but actually clean, in the way it bore on reality not at all, dealt in abstractions alone and corresponded to nothing. What parental relationship could that help you to understand, exactly? It only helped you to read books better, write better essays.

I wrote the essay. It received a High Distinction. It received a literary criticism award. I graduated, finally, in 2016, after five years. Just like Lacan.

*

Throughout the nineties, the coastal suburb of Swansea was the prime holiday destination for Sydney wogs of my ilk – or ırk, if you want the Turkish. We flocked in particular to a caravan park, one which has since been torn down and built back up into condos. It used to stand on the grass before one hit upon the fine blond sand of Caves Beach – which I ate without wanting to all those times Dilek pushed my face into the ground, and which tasted like nothing – and alongside hills covered in overgrown plants my father scaled once to pick us wild blackberries.

My sister and I sometimes spent the entire day on the verandah of our holiday cabin, sometimes with other family friends' kids, my father sat at a deck table smoking cigarettes in his tracksuit, recovering during daylight hours from his all-night fishing trips, and supervising us children cross-legged on the floor in a circle. We played a Turkish game called Yağ satarım, bal satarım, which involved hiding an old strip of fabric behind someone's back, as well as duck-duck-goose and piggy in the middle with me as the perpetual piggy.

The person who first taught me how to read was my mother, during the summer before I started kindergarten, in Swansea. In the evenings I lay in the bottom bunk of Dilek's and my bed with my mother. Her back against the cabin wall, propped up on a pillow, and me nestled into her side, we pored over a collection of five dinosaur books. She taught me by speaking out loud the words enough times that I memorised them, could recite each line by rote as soon as I spotted the dinosaur on the cover, like a sleeper agent triggered by stegosauruses. She hated the way I slowly caved into her while we read, leaning and leaning, before she would fold and shift away in annoyance, righting my body with both her hands, forcing me to sit up straight and support myself.

'Benim gibi zekisin sen,' said my mother, snapping a book shut in satisfaction, after I made no mistakes. 'It runs in the family. But just our women. Biliyor musun? Evvelsi gün babanız bana dinazorlar hala var mı diye sordu. Manyak herif ya.' She exhaled. 'Ama cahilliğe çare yok.'

I glanced at my father who was in earshot, dragging a bucket of freshly caught fish over the threshold of the open door, and felt a prick of shame about possessing knowledge which others didn't – about dinosaurs, about my father.

*

In kindergarten, my teacher, a middle-aged blonde, noted my academic ability. For a five-year-old, all that signified, I think, was that I knew the alphabet. Nevertheless, she took to keeping me in with her more lunchtimes than not. Together in a classroom of Marayong Public School we took test after test, which I usually filled out on the blank side of A2-size black-and-white drawings of animals intended for the other children to colour in. I completed the Waddington Test – which returned a reading age of eight years and nine months, three and a half years clear of my real age, and my mother showed the piece of paper to everyone – on the back of a zebra. I recall thinking I would have preferred to be colouring the zebra. They were already black and white, of course, though. What colour would I even add? I would take it home to play with later.

After, I walked into the school courtyard to salvage what was left of lunch, but all the kids in my class had already scattered. My teacher couldn't force any of them to treat me well, not to call me stinky for being ethnic or four eyes for wearing glasses – I had tiny spectacles before tiny spectacles were hip – and while I usually made do by sashaying into the senior quadrangle of the school grounds where I could find Dilek, and play with her friends, she had recently banned me from the exercise. The week before I had executed a study on whether one could engineer a friendship meet-cute by leaving a valuable belonging behind, in a classmate's eyeline, and seamlessly joining the life of whoever returned it. During lunchtime I had bought a chocolate crackle from the weekly cake stand thrown by the P&C, intentionally forgetting my wallet on the table. I stood watching from the classroom steps, like a chubby and myopic hawk, as a girl from class had picked it up and walked it over.

'You forgot this,' she said. I stood up.

'Can I have your hand in friendship?' I said, probably, already an insufferable wanker at age five, in my bespeckled spectacles.

'Yes,' she said – but we couldn't make it work.

It was autumn, so that day I made a game of chasing fallen leaves as they blew across the concrete quad, and counting how many I could catch underfoot, scoring based on colour: brown, orange, yellow, green the rarest and making the least satisfying crunch when trod upon. I recounted this story to my friend Tim, once, and he regularly cites it as one of the saddest stories he's ever heard – imagining a tiny me looking for ways to pass the time, all alone, designing games for herself. Although I have heard sadder stories, I find his sympathy validating.

Dilek had been deemed in need of an academic boost, so my mother and I took her to tutoring every Saturday in the lead-up to her departure into secondary school. The lessons were held in a classroom of Blacktown Girls High School, which was the local comprehensive that myself and my sister were under no circumstances to attend. Gülin had gone there before she even knew how to speak English. Dilek and I were born here – we had all the chances in the world to escape that fate.

My mother would set up a table – yellow, legs uneven, and graffitied with endless nineties fads like the special ℘ no one would teach me how to draw – in the hallway while we waited for Dilek, and my mother taught me how to read again, this time in Turkish.

'You're just like your great-great-grandmother,' she said once, after I spelled correctly the sentences she had given me, marking them with ticks. 'She was the first woman to learn to read the new alphabet after Atatürk introduced it, and be authorised to read the new Kuran. She had a certificate and everything.' She exhaled. 'Who knows what schools I could have gone to. I almost studied in France, you know. My teacher begged me not to let my talent go to waste, to go to France.'

Dilek emerged from the classroom then, wearing her backpack on her front like a big belly to tuck a manila envelope full of notes in, and tugging her ponytail out from under one of the straps. Her hair was much darker than mine and her nose much smaller and she didn't have an underbite. The pretty one between us, and esmer to boot, like my mother used to be pretty and esmer. My nickname, by contrast, was sarışın, for my fairer complexion. Or kumkum ağız, due to my preternaturally tiny mouth. Dilek and I were both also stupid bitches, ungrateful whores, dogs, thankless sons of bitches, too. Sometimes my kumkum ağız was an amcık ağız. But my mother was in a neutral mood on this day, so we remained esmer and sarışın.

We made off to Macca's Blacktown for lunch, and as we marched down Sunnyholt Road my mother explained to Dilek that the boys in her hometown used to call out, 'Türkân Şoray! Bak! Türkan Şoray geliyor!' as they scrambled out onto their balconies of a winter morning just to watch her walk past, in her wool skirt and long boots.

We visited Blacktown Library after, me picking up as many Emily Roddas as I could carry, all the Animorphs, the Catherine Jinkses (whom I would later meet when I worked as an arts administrator in Parramatta, and bond with over glasses of wine at an arts launch in Katoomba, two unfathomably wonderful things). Eventually I would kick on to the Fitzgerald-Orwell-Bradbury-Salinger adult-reading starter pack, and then Scott Card after Scott Card and K. Dick after K. Dick, and then King and Joyce and Forster and Knowles.

If I were to psychoanalyse myself, I would deduce that academic achievement, receiving a ninety-something on a test, was the only validation I could get my hands on, between the ages of five and nineteen. It delivered me the same little thrill each time with no attenuation. I had friends in the minutes that preceded tests and sometimes during, the length of time it took the other kids to copy my answers which I gave willingly. And it pleased my mother, who I have been trying to find the formula for pleasing for a long time, been studying for years the way to make her happy, to complete her, to ace her. Likewise I would describe reading as both an affirmation vehicle and a coping mechanism – the more I read, learned, and studied, the more elsewhere I was the more often, neither alone at lunchtime nor listening to my mother shout herself hoarse about the way we used her and used her up, and the less me and to-do-with-me things I contained.

Reading has always offered an exit route, a means of departing myself and my body, of not thinking about where or who I am, or myself as an 'I' whom I am driven to loathe. Academic achievement also represented a literal way out, provided I toiled hard enough. It gained me entry to an academically selective high school, for one. I was suicidal by the time I was ten, a feeling that was at its worst in Grade 7, and which kicked right on until my twenties. Due to the competitive nature of selective schools, the pressure, many of us struggled with mental illnesses. I mostly blended. By age thirteen, I was failing to shower most days. My longest streak, in the middle of a depressive episode, was two weeks without one, after which point I woke up suddenly at 3 am, skin too itchy to ignore, and scraped the loofah up and down my right arm, which is permanently discoloured by tinea versicolor, from all those months in the sun and water as a kid, and wondered what was wrong with me.

Years later, only when I am twenty-seven, and struggling

with the fact that I got so used to being utterly out of tune with my body that now, to compensate, I can't seem to stop body-scanning, processing every physical sensation that I experience as a symptom of a disease or a sign of my impending death – to make up for all the ways I ignored my body when I was young – do I figure out what was happening to me then and what is happening to me now.

At age fourteen, my tongue turned white one week and a bilious taste grew in the back of my throat and forced its way upward every few minutes, a stench that wouldn't go away no matter how much gum I chewed, and I thought I might finally cark it. The next week Google revealed I was just dehydrated – I had briefly forgotten to drink water or to register thirst as a need.

Fortunately, no one came close enough to sniff me out. I was hermetically sealed from the universe. Many selective school students are solipsists, in the sense that we are only brains, floating in jars, unable to afford to fuck or date or drink triple espressos before class like in teen movies – which, let's be real, would make even an adult shit their pants. We're busy!

We were booted from our Norfolk Street home the week that my Year 12 finals would take place, the intra-school exams that would precede the Higher School Certificate exams proper. We found a place, of course, on time, three streets down. But not before I had been caught by my English teacher in the library one day looking particularly morose – which was saying quite a bit, given when I was twelve and thirteen I could spend up to four hours fully prone on my couch, unable to move. In Grade 7 one of the more popular girls described me as 'moody' behind my back and when I found out I went home and cried, which was not a particularly robust debunking. My English teacher pulled out the plastic chair next to me and peeked at my monitor.

'Is everything okay, Eda?' I had quickly closed off the tab I had open on realestate.com.au, scrolling through listings to send to my parents because I couldn't attend the viewings myself. I explained that we had four days left in our house and my parents hadn't made plans, only conducted several arguments with the estate agent. My father had stopped paying rent a month in advance, his – in my view, genuinely clever and, indeed, anti-capitalist – tactic for ensuring there was no argument over getting the bond back or not at the end. I explained that I felt unsure about where I would be living soon, had considered staying with Melanie but that her parents could not take me.

She swung into action immediately – the way that all English teachers have somehow always acted as angels looking out for me – by organising for all of my trial examinations to receive a moderated mark if my perform-ance did slip, bringing any score I received up to where my rank in the class had already been sitting. I was called into the Year Adviser's office for the first time, a tough woman who I once saw physically kick a fellow male history teacher in his arse, friendly-like, but to get him to walk faster all the same.

'You're very resilient,' she said, after I explained some choice facts.

'Okay,' I said, feeling flattered – seen – but guilty. I felt shame over the whole affair, half-convinced I didn't deserve a moderation, that I had lied in some way, exaggerated the degree of difficulty, inadvertently faked everything. So I studied for trials more than I would have if none of it had happened. In between studying, I slept in the new house unfurnished, on a big red Elmo beanbag. Fortunately, I could study anywhere. Most days I could eke five hours out, from 6.30 pm to 11.30 pm. I studied from bed, hunched over my books which I scattered from bedhead to bedtoe. I was adept at forgetting I had a body, and so neckaches or the need for a toilet break were easy to ignore. I didn't notice if I was uncomfortable. It's not that there was some need there that I ignored – I simply did not know what it felt like to register pain, and I certainly didn't believe that, if I was in pain, there was anything I could do, or care enough about myself to do, to solve it.

When the school year ended and we moved onto stuvac, I ramped up. The boxes in my new bedroom remained unpacked for years, great big boxes full of unfolded clothes filled hurriedly. For the month leading up to the HSC I studied for thirteen hours every day, staying up till 3 or 4 am, powering against the parts of my brain which screamed, incessantly, you have to kill yourself, you have to. For study breaks, I read Ayn Rand's magnum opus, her 800-page tome *Atlas Shrugged*. I'm telling you, I could devour any bullshit that would serve as a distraction. I read it furiously, annotated it with a pen, as if my thoughts mattered.

*

I learned to love writing when I learned it made me leave my body. I started by writing suicide notes, which I seemed to enjoy drafting but could never quite perfect. That feeling of: *Is this the last thing I'm ever going to say? Is this? Or this? Is that meaningful enough? Does it sum it all up?* There was nothing *to* sum up. At some point that practice transformed into simply keeping diaries, and then to writing and end-lessly editing the garbage I wrote, restlessly and furiously going over the same sentence again and again. By Grade 11, I wanted to be a writer. I committed to writing a thousand words a day and soon I basked among a metric fuckbyte of trash, poor prose to do with people I wasn't, like white American males and terra-formed moons. In Year 11, I won the *Sydney Morning Herald* Young Writer of the Year award with a twee story about a dysfunctional family. Slippages. Spilling out. The writer Erik Jensen was a journo back then, and one of the judges. He pulled me aside after the awards ceremony, in the State Library of NSW, and in a dark corner by the stone bust of an old white man, he fast-talked some of the kindest things I had heard up until that point.

'You know, your work reminds me of David Foster Wallace's,' he said.

I took this as a compliment at the time. I felt that little thrill again, a bigger version, like a heroin-size hit of validation. I purchased all of Wallace's books. At the awards ceremony my mother drank two glasses of wine and cried. The journo who wrote the puff piece about me for the *Herald* wrote that my mother's tears were a signifier of pride. I am not sure what they signified: there are multiple interpretations available, some more generous than others. Before the journo took me into a corner of the Reading Room to be interviewed on my achievement, my mother leant in and reminded me to let him know my mother was a writer, too. We were well matched in a way, him and I; he was by far the oddest man I can recall ever meeting, shier than even me who was congenitally socially anxious. He held a recorder up to my face for every answer, his hand shaking every time. He asked me my favourite authors and I found myself saying embarrassing things like Thomas Mann and Kurt Vonnegut, laughing when I rambled, insisting that certain answers were 'off the record' as if I were a celebrity.

A week later we were in my father's ute, on the way to a dinner. My win was deemed a celebratory occasion, and so we were venturing to Rouse Hill, a more bourgeois part of the area because of its relative newness – in Western Sydney, fresh suburbs with gentle names to do with flora and fauna had a way of springing up in what had been, when I was younger still, empty fields, populated with the occasional statue of a cow. Simulacra of cows. We cruised up Sunnyholt Road.

My father's ute was older than me, still bearing a tape-deck, on which he used to listen to his folk music cassettes; manual locks and gears; and brown pleather torn in places. Instead of using seat covers or cushions, my father furnished the car with old pillows from dining chairs, which had lost half their stuffing, been thrown out and then salvaged. He gripped his knuckles on the steering wheel, not white because he is not white, but tight all the same, while my mother explained to me that her psychologist had suggested she put me in foster care for all my acting out. I was not the type of kid to act out, unless you counted not showering, catatonic sitting, et cetera. I said, from the backseat, loud so as to be heard over the wind rushing in through the open windows, which we wound down by hand, 'Can you not ruin today for me?'

And my mother snapped back faster than she had ever responded to me before, 'Why not? You ruined my life.'

My mother had her first kid at seventeen, under circumstances I didn't understand until I was twenty-five. By the end of the car ride she denied the comment had ever been made. I checked with Dilek, who was in the car, and she refused to confirm that it had been said. My father was too busy cranking the gears furiously, working the stick shift like he was starting a lawnmower.

Of course, all this shit happened before I knew any names for these occurrences. Instead, I felt acutely a sense that my mind had been overtaken by some kind of encroaching madness. I felt sure I would lose my mind, be carted off in an ambulance, like others in the family before me, before I met any goals or felt what joy felt like. To treat the feeling, I wrote constantly and urgently, able only to know what had happened the day before the next day because I had committed it to paper. These memories had a way of self-effacing, otherwise, simply evaporating into the air to protect me from themselves. Derrida calls that 'writing under erasure', something which exists and does not exist in an attempt to say the unsayable, which is itself.

I wrote in a small pink journal with a twee little lock on it all throughout high school. I called it my Suicide Diary, and thought it was ironic and amusing that it was pink and girlish and childish and contained such darkness. Erik was right that I am like David Foster Wallace but not in the best way. I write in my diary, later on that night, when we have come back from dinner, that I am afraid I will never become a writer because she would always destroy it, find some way to ruin my aspirations, to step on it and shit on it and shit on me. She makes you crazy and then asks why you're crazy, I wrote.

A week on from the incident in the car I came home from school and walked into my bedroom in the Norfolk Street house. This home was just down the road from the child psychologist I went to briefly, when I was twelve and newly suicidal. This psychologist's name was Natalie and she often had me write on a whiteboard, endless practices of learning to assign each of my thoughts to one of eight categories: black and white thinking, catastrophising, shoulds, over-generalisation, jumping to conclusions, personalisation and minimisation. After our five approved sessions she requested a conference with my mother, while I hung back in the waiting room. After, the psychologist told me that I had to respond to CBT, to stop being resistant to her treatment or not to renew my mental health care plan. She asked me when I would start taking over the housework, pitching in more with chores: this had been my mother's key grievance.

If I were to psychoanalyse my mother, which I do,

endlessly, trying, usually, to formulate the most generous reading possible, I would argue this. I would argue that she just wanted us to be treated the way that she herself had been. The youngest of four brothers, my mother started completing all of her household's domestic duties at age seven. If she didn't do them right, she was beaten. When I was growing up, she would ask either myself or my sister for a glass of water, and upon our return from the kitchen, my mother would always be sure to check our mouths to see if they were wet – if we had had a drink before giving her hers. She told us her father had beaten her for drinking before him, the lone time she did it.

Stepping into the house the week after the Young Writer incident, my bed was made though I never made it. I spotted a copy of *Dünya*, a local Turkish-language newspaper, on the ink-stained bedspread. On the cover was me, accompanying an article about my winning the *Herald*'s competition. My mother had used my Year 12 school photo. I had been sweating especially hard the day it was taken, so much so that I had needed to step into the bathroom and peel off my shirt to dry it out, and had stood topless for a few beats while I tried to breathe through the summer. In the school photo, my hair was visibly oily, grimy. I looked – was – dirty, dishevelled. I don't remember much about what followed – my head heated up in that crazy way that will be mine to grapple with forever, and so I did not write the incident, or anything much else, for a long time, down. I do remember that I binned the copies of the newspaper, which my mother had laid out to surprise me with. In the face of my ingratitude, later, my mother asked me, 'Why are you acting like this?' And God, wouldn't it have been funny if I responded, 'Mother, I learned it from you?'

There are multiple interpretations available for why my mother had my face put in that paper. My teenage self felt sure she knew how ugly I felt that day, wanted to mock me, wanted others to join in laughing about the thin layer of grime that coated her daughter. Rather, my teenage self felt hurt that her mother could not see the untreated mental illness that caused said daughter to end up so grimy in the first place. The critic in me wants to say that my mother only wanted to claim my achievement as her own, and compensate for some of her unachieved literary and professional goals. Or, I want to say that she used me in order to show off, and enhance her value inside her community which was not my community. Sometimes, though, I wonder about a third dimension, a less partial reading. I wonder if she was also just trying to make up for her comment about my ruining her life, if maybe she was only trying to redeem herself. That would be the reparative reading, the alternate angle to take, if I let myself take it. I know it would make me happier.

Live On

'It's basically empty!' says Tim of my spare room. We're both looky-loos. He's touring the house, although he's been here many times – we meet every Tuesday evening to play a game of chess and catch up, and alternate between eating cheese and singing loudly and tunelessly along to *The Smiths, Charli XCX, The Mountain Goats*. He holds out his arms to assess the size of the space, then turns back to look at me. 'You could totally fit a baby in here!'

I mime shooting myself in the head.

After we play, and I win, I collect my prize. We have a sort of sick agreement that if I beat him – this is my first and, so far, last time – I get to hear an entry from his diary. I collect with delight, learning from a few off-handed sentences that he is better at chess than he is with money.

'Hey! It's so much harder to track your spending when your accounts are shared,' he says. 'All of mine are shared, whereas you and Justin have a very different system.' He's right: Justin and I shuffled money spent on shared expenses

206

back and forth like day traders. Partially inertia around admin and partially something else. 'You two won't even cook for each other.'

My mind jumps to the woman that lived in Tire, my mother's hometown, who walked up into the mountains surrounding the town almost every day to forage for food; her husband wouldn't provide any. My mind jumps to my mother at a dinner with her parents and her first husband, age eighteen. My mother's father has just asked her to help cover the cost of the meal, which she can't do. The power goes out suddenly, so she thinks on her feet: reaches into her husband's wallet under cover of darkness and pulls out 50 lira. When he asks later if she's seen it, she tells him he must have gambled it away.

I want to say it's not cute to depend on others. Instead I shrug, and say, 'We have different palates.'

*

There's a store on Parramatta Road that I walk past daily on my way to work, often at the same time that one of the staff is opening up; we share a choreography of labour. She steps out, holding an A-Frame, and props it open with a click, leaving it by the door, and it advertises some product they are selling: a microscope or a life-like doll. The store is a toy shop called KIDSTUFF. Every time I pass it I think of Lee Edelman, a joke that a few queer theorists might get but not find funny. *The future is kid stuff.*

And so, perhaps contrary to their intentions, every day I pass the store I think about not only not wanting toys but also not wanting kids. In his 2004 book, *No Future: Queer Theory and the Death Drive*, Edelman writes:

> Why not acknowledge our kinship at last with the Scrooge who, unregenerate, refuses the social imperative to grasp futurity in the form of the Child, for the sake of whom, as the token of accession to Imaginary wholeness, everything else in the world, by force if needed, must give way?

I think, perhaps patronisingly, that a lot of people want a child because they've seen it go right, and haven't seen it go wrong. It's like driving a car. How so? Well, it's two things I can't do. But what I also mean is that these are fears that are analogous, treated with the same variety of probabilistic reassurance that most of the time it's fine. Only the unlucky few roll a freak accident.

Cars race by on my left every day, and it's true that I've never witnessed a collision. Still, I don't get my licence. I hate those odds – only normies are soothed by those odds. I'm perfectly content with my death drive, thank you. Another joke one might get but not find funny.

*

I pass my landlord on the street, by chance. I stop with him and we talk, although I am meant to be in a hurry – I hope my lanyard, swinging round my neck, might project the working gal air that I am unable to. He shows me pictures of his grandchildren. I coo at appropriate moments, conjure up suitable statements like, 'Oh, she likes pink!' while I smile.

At work I greet an admin officer and we chat briefly in the elevator. I pass two colleagues in the halls, and we discuss their weekends. I stop by another colleague's office: I have offered to walk her puppy, which I spend the next half-hour doing. She roams the grounds of the campus (the puppy, not the colleague), bounding into patches of grass and clovers, tangling herself into the legs of passers-by, and snuffling through her flat nose. I return her, log onto an organising meeting for casualised university staff, and then check my phone. My mother and father have both called and texted, my father alternating between WhatsApp and Facebook messenger. 'Please,' he's written. 'Call mummy. She needs you.'

I glean that they are requesting that I make my mother a neurologist appointment, as a matter of urgency. They've left it late and she needs to see someone, now. I recall issuing a specific warning on this subject, the day we stepped out of a different specialist's office at the Royal North Shore Hospital a month prior. Before the appointment, I had stood outside the Kolling Building waiting for my father's ute to pull into the car park. Noticing that the O in Kolling had dropped off, I snapped a photo. 'An infelicitous letter to have fall off a building at a hospital,' I wrote, and uploaded it to Twitter.

The second time I stood out front of the hospital, the mood was different, my mother feeling disregarded by the orthopaedic surgeon. In the office he had laid her down and inspected her like a warm carcass, rotating bits of her body and ignoring her complaints about how little she had to live for, how she couldn't brook the idea of another surgery this year, how she wasn't sure she could get through four more joint replacements. The surgeon, whom I despise, had ignored her, turned to his assistant and murmured, 'So, no surgery then,' and dropped into his chair at his desk, muttering concluding remarks into his tape recorder. I supposed I could admire that he recognised the limits of his use: no surgery, no surgeon. My mother had lain there, prone, unaware that the examination had ended, until I had snapped, 'Can she get up?'

He ignored me, but his assistant responded yes, and I heaved my mother to her feet, helped her put her shoes back on. After the surgeon had sauntered from the room, the assistant had remarked, 'A bit teary today, isn't she, your mum?' I had explained about her anti-epileptic medication, and her neurologist's unwillingness to take her suicidal ideation seriously enough to put her on something else. The assistant, Kim, had given me the name of her personal neurologist, who had helped her son through something similar. I wrote down the name and walked my mother out to the front of the KILLING BUILDING so she could stand crying.

'Don't forget it's the levetiracetam doing this,' I had said. 'You can't trust how you feel all the time. Yes, your circumstances are bad, but you might feel just a little bit better, a bit stronger, if we switched medications. Neurologist appointment bu gün yapsak iyi olur.' I pulled out my phone; my Tweet had twelve likes.

'Onu düşünemem şimdi,' she said, and then tugged on my sleeve. 'Hadi kahve içelim.'

At the cafe we sipped burnt coffee, our face masks pulled

below our chins, tugging on our ears. My mother begged me to come sleep over that evening.

I insisted that İşim var, the only reasonable excuse I am afforded or that I afford myself. I have to catch up on the work I have missed being here. She pleaded again, so I finally broke off, 'No, I don't fucking want to.'

My mother stopped crying, tried another way in.

'I don't know why Kim said that I'm lucky to have you as my advocate before,' she remarked. Kim had said it as we exited: Don't worry, Mum, you're in good hands. 'She doesn't know what you really are.'

*

It was my first day at a new school, Grade 5. My mother arrived in the afternoon to pick me up as a one-off, to help me locate the bus stop I would be using to travel home from then on. She collected me from outside the classroom, taking my hand into her grip. I shook it loose – was anxious to get out of sight of my new classmates, whom I had failed to befriend. During recess, I had walked up to a group of girls seated in a circle. Walked up, walked away; walked up, walked away. Couldn't summon the nerve to speak to anyone. A third party observing might have thought I had a murder to confess to, or a note to hand over taking them all hostage on a small plane I had stolen.

My mother and I moved, without holding hands, in a random direction, got ten metres across the grounds before she looked down at me and asked, 'Where is the bus stop?', and I, still embarrassed, or bitter or disappointed with myself, responded, ungenerously, 'How am I supposed to know?' And she bit off the phrase nankör köpek and took off, while I roamed the grounds searching for a way home, crying; she reappeared later, my teacher beside her, both of them confused, or acting confused, about why it had been me who walked off.

The same year, but summer. We stayed at a motor inn off the side of the highway in Swansea. My father brought us back KFC for lunch, which we ate on a plastic outdoor dining set by the pool – wrapped in towels, reapplying sunscreen while peeling the skin off chicken with our hands, making the chips soggy with droplets coming off our hair. My mother closed off a box that was half-full, moved it to the corner of the table so that family friends, when they arrived, could eat something too. But I wanted more chicken – probably, I think, kicked up a fuss. And she called me a nankör köpek and walked away, this time locking herself in the bathroom for several hours. In between sobs and muffled shouting, she let me know she'd thrown up the food she ate, and was I happy? My father asked me to apologise. I did, pleading from behind the door, and we came home early, ended the trip, lost what we'd paid on the room.

High school. I finally had friends, stable friendships. I liked to arrange elaborate gifts on their birthdays. One year I organised a scavenger hunt; another year I baked a small, disappointing croquembouche, burning myself repeatedly with caramelised sugar but kept going back in like a hungry rat. In return, on my birthdays, I received a painting; a reproduction of a Harry Potter book, printed at home, rewritten to place me into the action; handmade cards. The exchanges peeved my mother, and I took to making trips to the store for supplies in secret. The times that I told her where I was going and what I had planned, she'd throw up a fuss. Raise her voice at the shopping centre, causing other shoppers to start granting us an ever-widening berth: Enayi yerine koyuyorlar seni. Kullanılıyorsun. Sizin beni kullandığınız gibi. You're being used, just the way you use me.

*

I read the text message, 'Call mummy.' I can't call mummy. I'm sorry. Or I won't. I would rather walk into traffic than call mummy. I call mummy. I restore her will to live. I don't say, 'Seni uyardım' and I don't say, 'No, I won't email the neurologist and beg for an emergency appointment.' I do it, and I do it, and then I go home and sit in a dark room because I feel like I have been struck by a truck, my face numb from a familiar tension headache. I feel like panting, although I have accomplished nothing that was on my to-do list today. What was I thinking, giving away all my energy? Am I motherfucking Pippi Longstocking, roaming the face of the planet casting about in search of someone, anyone, in need of do-gooding?

My mother has started using a new nickname for me: Florence Nightingale, she calls me, after I've bought her a new pain cure or dealt with endless reams of medical paperwork or brought over soup, or, in this instance, right before we hang up the phone and her mood has improved. Although it's better than others, the name makes me cringe.

*

My psychologist has no time for my driving phobia. When I raise it, she laughs.

'No, Eda,' she says. She rejects these low-hanging forms of dysfunction. They make me feel basic when I raise them, like I need to bring out the big trauma guns only – earn my spot here in her office. It's my own hang-up. 'Anyone can drive. I can't be clearer about this. If billions of people of varying levels of intellect and attention-span can drive, so can you.'

'My mother can't drive,' I try. My mother's nerves are too frayed to have ever learned. The handful of instances she had attempted it she had driven each time into a ditch. She wants us to drive, though, tries to goad us into learning. For my twenty-third birthday she gave me a card that read: 'CONGRATULATIONS ON YOUR DRIVER'S LICENCE!' I did not have one. Inside, she had written the note: 'I read somewhere that parents who spend a lot of time with their children have longer lifespans.' Beneath that: 'So that's how I know you want me to die.'

'Anyone can drive,' says my psychologist.

I see her eyes flick the corner of the room. Psychologists always keep their clocks in discreet nooks, as if we can't tell that we have lost their gaze. I am sensitive to these minor, perceived rejections, although I am trying not to be, in order that I may feel less obligated to protect others from perceiving rejection from me, when I do something like check my watch during a conversation and hope the other person doesn't accuse me of hating their company, or saying 'I have to go' when I have to go. I nod so vigorously and quirk my eyebrows and generally emote so much when others speak, to show that I am listening, that co-panellists at writers' festivals have asked me if I'm okay: once it had been so exaggerated that they thought I was being sarcastic. Some nights, while drifting to sleep, I find myself smiling or frowning and furrowing or raising my brows reflexively in response to the conversations being staged by the characters in my oncoming dreams. Through various acts of conversational jiu jitsu I flip conversations around. Now we're talking about you, and you like it that way, don't you, arsehole? My mother, once, hadn't known how to get off the phone with Gülin who kept talking and talking, unaware my mother had to use the bathroom. She had silently pissed herself. The family cycle: locked into patterns of fawning that make it impossible to separate out what part of oneself contains the presence or absence of a genuine ethic of care.

'Fine,' I say, throwing up my hands. 'Okay, great. I can drive.' *Vroom, vroom*, I think sarcastically. But I do indeed start to learn, a few weeks later. We have half an hour remaining – I had thought the question of whether I could drive might take a little longer to unpack – so I cast about for something juicier. 'Does it make me like my mother if I find myself keep repeating the cycle of giving something – doing someone a favour, or letting them tell me all their trauma – and then feeling resentful about it later? Am I an un-giving person?'

'Maybe,' she says. I had wanted her to say something else. 'But why do you feel so convinced you need to be like your mother?'

*

The idea of the tainted bloodline sits somewhere between epigenetics and eugenics. For all the work done post-Holocaust exploring the ways that trauma in the blood-line can lead to inheritance of an altered physiology – heightened cortisol levels, hypertension, shortened life-spans – there is a growing body of work that questions both the nature and extent of this impact, specifically how it has been distorted and simplified in public discourse. The idea that memories can be inherited, for example, is widely discredited. They can be passed down, certainly, but only through immanent processes: re-tellings, collective memory, oral history.

As Alana Lentin writes in her 2020 *Why Race Still Matters*, 'There is always the potential for the findings of epigenetics research and the idea of biological plasticity to be used to propose eugenics-type policies.' I am mistrustful of a science that tells us we can inherit our forebears' weaknesses without focusing on the ways we can inherit their strengths. So I must believe that dysfunctional behaviours aren't genetically encoded, predetermined. But maybe they are reproduced in the social: by the way we are treated and learn to treat ourselves and others. Material and social facts extend beyond biological ones: intergenerational cycles of poverty are more likely to shape health outcomes. Each generation can hold trauma but also do and be something other than that – not take its fact as a foreclosure. No, I'm not genetically marked out. When I say I want to end my bloodline, I don't mean that a child may inherit something from me – I mean that I may pass something on.

*

I drive Tim to Lalor Park to pick up a rug for his new place. It's forty-five minutes in both directions, and he pitches it to me on the phone with the rationale that it'll be good night-driving practice. I am trying to be giving without getting mad at the end. This requires understanding my own boundaries: that is, saying no, on occasion. So I weigh the request.

'You can get your hours up,' he says. I remind him, again, that I'm twenty-six: there are no hours. We're old enough to take responsibility for our shitty choices.

'What's the difference?' he says. 'You need to drive at night, don't you?'

'Fine,' I say, accepting the quid pro quo.

I enjoy driving: I find it to be a dissociative activity. My passengers don't like to hear this information. But it is a way to feel disembodied, to enter flow, and to exit awareness of one's own tedious, repetitive thoughts. We zoom down the M4 tunnel, me trying to contain a rising irritability at being confined in a space that, when you enter, insists that you are now responsible for supplying your own oxygen. I am explaining to Tim about a friend I used to have who lived near Lalor Park, Melanie. I would go to her house almost every day in my last two years of high school, and we'd spend hours talking about her life, over pizza. Or we might watch *The L Word* on her couch.

'But we weren't dating, crucially,' I say. 'In fact, she mainly told me about the people she *was* dating. Who weren't me.'

'Oh mate, I'm sorry,' says Tim. He's eating the blueberries I packed us as a snack, still in his suit from a long day at work. 'That seems like such a typical bisexual tale.'

'No, I mean,' I say, flick my indicator and look over my shoulder and change lanes to overtake the frustratingly slow vehicle in front of me. 'I don't mean to say I had romantic feelings for her.' I want to confiscate Tim's blueberries.

He laughs with disbelief.

'So why'd you spend so much time together?'

'I just – did it because she wanted me to, I guess. My feelings were sort of a moot point.'

'Which is insulting.'

'Which is insulting,' I intone. We exit the tunnel.

*

I've spent all this time reacting against the nuclear family, but it's gone ahead and collapsed itself already: tilting at windmills. In his 2009 book *Capitalist Realism: Is There No Alternative?*, Mark Fisher writes that

> The situation of the family in post-Fordist capitalism
> is contradictory, in precisely the way that traditional
> Marxism expected: capitalism requires the family (as
> an essential means of reproducing and caring for labor
> power; as a salve for the psychic wounds inflicted
> by anarchic social-economic conditions), even as it
> undermines it (denying parents time with children,
> putting intolerable stress on couples as they become the
> exclusive source of affective consolation for each other).

Justin and I joked with horror about the tactics parents had to develop during the pandemic, aimed at regulating their children's access to their time while they attempted to work from home. When I would wear a shawl in my cold office, set up in the spare room – in lieu of a crib – Justin joked that I was wearing my 'work scarf' and that he mustn't talk to me right then. We had read a Tweet from a mother who had adopted this practice with her son, the world's saddest stop light party. Neoliberalism has pushed at the edges of the social fabric and given us this: all labour and no relations.

I think, if they weren't already before, that these are not appropriate conditions to reproduce in. Even kangaroos get lay of the land before they decide to gestate. I'm grasping around in the past for a politic to hang my hat on. The Cathars, now wiped out, had refused the imperative to bring children into an evil world and condemn them to suffering. Of course, the Catholics didn't like this, but I think that neither does the modern left.

I understand the constellation of pro-procreation positions. For all the feminist movements that have prioritised the right to escape the domestic, and move into public life, there are others for whom the right to reproduce has been denied. Whereas white, middle-class women have been forced, in their position as keepers of the nation, to give birth, borders and punitive citizenship and carceral regimes deny Black and Brown people their families. The state continues to steal babies from parents' arms, and non-consensually sterilise the poor, the incarcerated, and Indigenous people,

When interpreted this way, anti-natalism is bourgeois, ableist, colonial. But my concern remains. A child might not ruin my life. I might ruin theirs.

In his foreword to the 2018 edition of *The Communist Manifesto*, Yanis Varoufakis quotes Marx when he says that we are now in the grip of a 'universal energy which breaks every limit and every bond and posits itself as the only policy, the only universality, the only limit and the only bond.' He writes that 'capitalism's reach is so pervasive it can sometimes seem impossible to imagine a world without it.'

I have witnessed, during this pandemic, suppressed child-rearing models proliferate out of necessity: members of the white, middle class are turning away from the old standbys of paying for au pairs, who no longer exist – in France they just call them exploited – or paying for childcare, which they can no longer afford. Instead, practices historically reserved for the poor, and Aboriginal people and people of colour, are popularising. Children spend more time with grandparents, older siblings, or are sent to neighbours' houses to be watched in groups by older members of the community, who may not be relatives at all.

So is it hopepunk to have a baby? To dare a new future to manifest itself, because it has to, it just has to, once we have something worth saving? To refuse nihilism, to refuse to annihilate oneself, to force alternative social relations to manifest?

*

When I was younger, my mother liked to have an audience when ironing. It was her most loathed domestic chore, so she distracted herself with chatter. She would flip and rotate our school uniforms or my father's polo shirts, skimming the iron over the fabric's surface in a hissing zig-zag, rounding collar corners smoothly, and explain how and why she became so expert at the task.

'Erkut beni öyle bir döverdi ki,' she would say. Her first husband was a major in the army – all Turkish men are expected to serve twenty-four months. 'Eğer üniformasını yeterince iyi ütülemeysedim. Çenemi kırdı bir kere.' She would look up. 'Senin kocanda bir gün ütü yapmanı bekler.'

In her 2019 book *Full Surrogacy Now: Feminism Against Family,* Sophie Lewis writes that,

> We simply cannot generalize about 'the social' without
> knowing the specifics of the labor itself. And, regardless
> of the 'ground' the gestational relationship provides, the
> fabric of the social is something we ultimately weave
> by taking up where gestation left off, encountering
> one another as the strangers we always are, adopting
> one another skin-to-skin, forming loving and abusive
> attachments, and striving at comradeship. To say
> otherwise is to naturalize and thus, ironically, to devalue
> that ideological shibboleth 'the mother-fetus bond.'
> What if we reimagined pregnancy, and not just its
> prescribed aftermath, as work under capitalism – that
> is, as something to be struggled in and against toward a
> utopian horizon free of work and free of value?

*

I am experimenting with defining for myself what care outside of gender and capitalism – if such a thing were possible – might look and feel like. When I walked with a student after class and checked in with them to see if they were doing all right, they looked at me with tears in their eyes and thanked me for asking. And when I phoned a friend after the death of their parent and we spoke, later they said thank you for knowing things to say (most people don't know what to say). Both of these instances felt like work – an intentional, practised labour – but they did not feel like I was being used.

Lee Edelman and Mark Fisher both write about the film *Children of Men,* which I and most white men love. Fisher interprets the film's theme of sterility as a metaphor for the cultural sterility we find ourselves embroiled in, living in an era that cannot imagine a future outside of, or alternatives to, capitalism, and which has therefore become incapable of generating something new. He focuses on one of the opening scenes of the movie, a character who sits in a room full of preserved private art pieces, lamenting that there are no more generations to enjoy them. Edelman, on the other hand, interprets the film as a classic redemption narrative. He focuses on the final scene of the movie, in which the main character births a miracle baby, the first infant born in eighteen years – the possibility of the future of the social order as we know it tied to this act. But they overlook the best scene of the film, widely regarded by cinematographers as the 'miracle ceasefire scene'. In the middle of the movie, during a long take in which the protagonist runs through a refugee camp, dodging bullets and explosions, a random accident, not planned by the auteur, causes droplets of blood to splatter over the camera's lens, producing flares that soften the shot in places. The directors, rather than calling cut, kept on rolling, and rolling. I am interested in these previously unimagined-until-they-happen moments. They remind me that we cannot anticipate much of anything – I have taken to remarking to Tim that, although I used to worry, incessantly, I don't anymore, because at no point this year have I known what would take place either in my personal life and world-historically. We keep remarking to each other that these are *unprecedented times* – following a mass-death event, neoliberalism is being tested, the global political economy has started to burst at the seams, inequality is at a fever pitch. Unprecedented times are what precede revolutions. Meanwhile, where Justin and I used to discuss how we might like to have kids, if I ever changed my mind – through surrogacy, adoption, biological childbirth – now we only speak over emails that I sign off with *Warmly,* and I shrug when I think about mothering, leaving the question for some future Eda to answer. My insistence on not trying to think too many steps ahead makes me a newly (even more) terrible chess player. Tim wants to pull out his hair with competitiveness, I think, sometimes, when I kick back mid-game and simply remark, 'Eh, I'm just gonna let it play out. Maybe something good will happen.'

Tell-all

I could tell you
If I wanted to,
What makes me
What I am.

But I don't
Really want to –
And you don't
Give a damn.

– Langston Hughes, *Impasse*

Another abandoned book project of mine is a memoir, which is not like this book at all: it omits nothing, says everything, or most of it, and the narrative starts from the start of the story and goes till the end. I stopped writing it two years ago. Not for lack of interest, but for lack of understanding, maybe. I shit you not, I have seen things you people wouldn't believe. But why should I tell anyone about it? I stopped because I realised that forcing someone to look at me is no guarantee that I will be seen. How could I write about, say, my experience with a cult that abused and traumatised a loved one, among tens of others, culminating in a court case in which the offender was acquitted, and the complainants victim-blamed publicly? How could I, when I am steeped in a culture which views cults as a joke: something to meme, or dedicate a season of a tween TV show to, or an episode of a podcast to, or to make into merchandise?

I listen to true crime podcasts because I am obsessed with trauma – like picking at a scab. I am so scabby that in order to access a podcast's online-only content, I pay to register as a member of the 'Fan Cult'. As an unwanted reward for my purchase(s), I have received a pin, a t-shirt, and a hat, bearing that phrase. I can barely look at these items, let alone wear them. It's humourless of me. When I was younger I would hang out on Omegle (text-only), chatting to strangers, and once one of my interlocutors wrote, 'I seek to understand, whereas you wait to be understood', and then our connection was lost.

A friend who is a memoirist and I talk about the compulsion to disclose, over drinks at the Commercial Hotel in Parramatta. She is just about to publish her memoir, and she prods me to hurry up and finish mine. We agree to meet up here in this same place again in exactly two years and discuss my book the same way we have just done with hers: unpacking our anxieties about saying certain things publicly for the first time. I even make a show of slotting the date into my calendar, holding my phone's screen up facing outwards to show her. But I suspect I won't really do it, and nor – angry this time, at no one and myself – can anyone make me. You can poke and prod me but I ain't squealing.

And yet. Like her, I want to make disclosures, endlessly. I want to build intimacies to overcome the sense that this is so fucking mundane, that we, freshly emotionally regulated, full-time job holding perfect subjects of neoliberalism, are now trapped in a prison of pretending like we don't want to talk incessantly about one of three things: trauma, sex and anti-capitalism. Are we ever thinking about anything but these things? The way that any sleepover builds this heterotopic space which devolves and opens up necessarily into a conversation about fucking. The way that every game of Never Have I Ever is about fucking. The way that we all want to say to each other what the worst thing we've ever done is, and be forgiven.

On the true crime podcast I listen to, one of the hosts – whom I love and adore – does a bit which sends the other host, without fail, into peals of laughter.

'Shhhhh,' she slurs. 'Let me – I wanna tell you a secret,' acting drunk, and you just know, although you can't see her, that she is imitating leaning over real close to you at a bar. 'Can I just – lemme tell you a secret. I wanna tell you a secret.'

The Political Function of Confession

It feels like a breakthrough when I make certain disclosures to new friends I am getting to know, people I have been dating for a few weeks and am starting to feel comfortable around, imagined readers who I fantasise about finding my work relatable. But then I regret them. The topic changes and I feel more alone. This pattern has taught me that not every impulse must be honoured, and that communicating authentically and communicating intentionally are not mutually exclusive. I have learned this through years spent practising scripts for healthy communication, and have even stuck a list of 'Reality Statements for Interpersonal Effectiveness' on my bedroom wall, which include that 'I have a choice to ask someone for what I want or need' or that 'I sometimes have a right to assert myself, even though I may inconvenience others'. I also know that sometimes it is better to stay silent, and that speaking can't help every situation. So why, in these lapsed moments, does it feel right? There is a visceral emphasis placed on unburdening oneself; getting it off your chest; on letting it out; on spewing, spilling, blabbing, slipping; spitting it out; shitting it out; on reaching catharsis.

In *The History of Sexuality*, Michel Foucault writes of confession, the disclosure of one's inner-most truths, as one of the modern technologies of the self. Since its invention, which Foucault traces to the thirteenth century, western subjects have used confession to produce truths about themselves. Confession has increasingly replaced a prior reliance on others – family and community – to vouch for us, making the rise of the confession coextensive with the modern rise of the individual. Outside of the church, the obligation to confess permeates additional quarters of society in increasingly secular forms: inside of scientific discourses such as medicine (if you've ever filled out a mental health questionnaire, or pulled down your pants to show a rash, or tried to donate blood but been denied); in the world of work (self-evaluations of performance; enumerating our agendas and goals; accounting for the perceived breaks in one's career); in psychoanalysis; in literature, namely memoir; and through mediated communication such as social media.

That confession is widespread does not mean it is, to paraphrase Chloe Taylor in her book *The Culture of Confession From Augustine to Foucault*, an innate psychological need or a natural longing of the soul. That truth feels as if it demands to surface requires us to question the forces that make it feel this way. Speaking the truth cannot be inherently liberating inside a relation of power. I say this for two reasons. The first is that to confess is to transform something previously non-discursive into discourse. The second is that to speak is to open the self up to the external force of the witness: the one that, Foucault writes, plays the role of hearing and interpreting the confession, taking up the role of the master of truth, and using this power over the penitent to govern their behaviour.

As Capital is my Witness

Leave me alone, please. I'm very happy. I know I'm a good potter; I know that the stores, the good ones, like what I do. Does everything have to be on a great scale, with a cast of thousands? Can't I lead my little life the way I want to?

– *Flow my Tears, the Policeman Said*, Philip K Dick

Saul Newman describes social media as a 'mass confessional space'. He writes, 'Today there is such an excess of confessional behaviour, such an overexposure of the private to the public, that the very notion of the confession – that which reveals what is most hidden and intimate, and therefore what is supposedly most significant to the individual – has almost lost all meaning.' On the internet, another name for confession is *over-sharing*, and it has become synonymous with how we use social media platforms. People can't get a hold of me over text, but they can just read my tweets: it's all there, every beat of my mental state.

I may never tell you in person that I last cried at work in February, or that my parents have $3000 to their name and that concerns me greatly, or that I think that I look like I have a five o'clock shadow in certain lighting, or that my mother's chronic illness makes me feel miserable all the time, or that I recently lay on the floor because I was too burnt out to get up, or that I missed *MasterChef* on 29 June because I was helping my mother through a panic attack, but that *MasterChef* is what stops me from having a panic attack. But, somehow, these are all things I posted in the past week. Writing these tweets has surely helped me cope: in therapeutic terms, they are the canoe that helped me safely travel from one side of the river to the other. But now that I have reached the next shore, it might be time to build myself a better boat. In other words, I wonder if my over-sharing functions as a half-measure. I am worried that this is a way of pantomiming a level of comfort with vulnerability that I actually lack; that I am screaming into the void without having to receive any feedback. Or, put another way, I fear that to over-share is to seek out the rewards of being loved without submitting to the mortifying ideal of being known. Letting friends who see my tweets seek me out rather than asking someone in particular for support directly, and risking having this need, now articulated, go unmet. Dropping a tweet thread but committing to not reading the replies. Posting anonymously on my throwaway so I can say everything.

*

Identity formation under these circumstances is newly fraught. When did I learn to check if I exist by asking a machine? The map tells me I am a being in space. The clock tells me I am a being in time. The astrology app tells me I am a Sagittarius. David Lynch's Ominous Statement Generator tells me, 'The caves cannot reach you. Sleep well: they, too, have teeth.' And this has also been a form of telling on myself: now you know my birthdate, my eye colour, my birth order and my hair colour. All this self, staged publicly.

These are frivolous examples, but they do suggest to me a relative decline in older ways of being known or making oneself known: in the private sphere, one-on-one, in ongoing dialogue with individuals known to me and who form part of my community, who form part of my network of accountability, and who, more than anyone else, should get to witness, vouch for, and provide input on who I am. Astrology is a secular technology of the self that purports to supply deep insights about who we are. As it undergoes a modern renaissance, I have had two birth charts made for me: one by a good friend in an Airbnb on a weekend away in the Blue Mountains, just the two of us, as she explained what my chart may mean cross-referenced and improved against what she knew about me, Eda. The other was made by an AI, which sends me garbled push notifications every week. One is thrillingly impersonal, and the other almost unbearably intimate. For me, I wonder if tweeting replaces seeking out the company of friends or my therapist because it's a lot less uncomfortable than making an appointment, commuting forty minutes, sitting in an enclosed and unfamiliar space, fully embodied, and making eye contact for sixty straight minutes while my arse gets read.

To confess is to transform desire into discourse. Each of my Google searches produces into the world a piece of data about myself and thus charts a desire. I have told on myself again, by telling the algorithm what I want. My use of domain. com.au and realestate.com.au indicate that lately I want to move house. The advertisements for Curable on Facebook tell me that I want a solution to my mother's chronic pain. The advertisements for language learning platforms tell me that I want to get so fluent in Turkish that my parents and I never misunderstand each other again. And they also tell me what I should want, or things I want that I didn't know I wanted: to be pregnant (but still find time to work out); to manicure my nails and dye and style my hair (rather than avoiding these services religiously, and having friends give me trims); to be comfortable wearing shorts (belted); or to wear more deodorant (admittedly not a bad suggestion).

My desires are sublimated and sold back to me in the form of products. I can't buy my way out of these sensations: of bearing witness to the suffering of others; of how I feel about my body; of uncertainty around the management of difficult relationships; of contemplating what sort of parent I may or may not go on to make. But I can tell you I'll never wear shorts.

These disclosures are largely involuntary. Without our knowledge, when we go online, we have become workers, producing, in the words of Jodi Dean, 'information, services, relations and networks' for a handful of tech CEOs who own the platform. Most importantly, we produce data, which is sold at the highest profit margin possible, extracted from us for free, sold to others, and later used to induce purchases through targeted advertisements. The products of our virtual labour do not belong to us. Indeed, the majority of us do not even know what information has been sold to whom, or for what price. It is for this reason that Dean states that all of us who work in the knowledge economy, or even just use the internet, are 'proletarianized under communicative capitalism'. That might be the case, but it's still worth every second of immiseration to know what my personalised David Lynch Ominous Statement is.

Communicative capitalism has gone on to replace the scientific establishment, which Foucault critiqued, as the most significant repository of our confessions. I am much more likely to Google my symptoms than to consult a doctor as a first measure, although I live in a country with decent access to healthcare. Many of us have accidentally or otherwise made a worrying enough search to trigger the number for Lifeline at the top of our screens: this is the computer telling us we are not doing okay, and have thought something so unhealthy that it is actually a symptom, perhaps of depression or an eating disorder. During the height of the Ebola pandemic in West Africa, tracing of the disease allegedly took the form of surveilling private text messages for suspicious missives that indicated that a citizen might be symptomatic or ill. Likewise, in South Korea, during the COVID-19 crisis, reams of individuals' data were released to facilitate contact tracing. The witness of the truths of our bodies is these algorithms, which pick us out and diagnose us. While these measures are implemented in the name of public health, it is unlikely that algorithms can escape the racist and sexist biases of their creators. For example, big data has been used in 2020 to identify regions of the US and Australia that contain higher or lower numbers of infractions of public health orders regarding COVID-19 – high levels of movement gleaned from location data, for example – but without attention to the social and material conditions that make it impossible for poorer people to stop leaving their houses and travelling to their places of work. In July of 2020, thousands of poor, mostly Black, former refugees, and/or formerly incarcerated individuals were trapped by the police in social housing units in Melbourne. Meanwhile, such technologies have not been applied to single out and criminalise the wealthy – businesspeople, politicians, celebrities, millionaires and billionaires – such as those who fled to second homes when the crisis began, or readily crossed borders that are closed to others. These disparities that exist between those who do and do not receive dispensations from the requirement to confess demonstrate that only some of us are sick, while others get to be rich.

It Happened to Me

Once, when the tape recorder was finally off, a child survivor said to Gordon, 'I know what you want from me but you are not going to get it even if you sit here all day.'

– Maria Tumarkin, *Axiomatic*

Confessional writing has existed for longer than we have had a name for it. Preceding the rise of capital, but not the church, St Augustine's *Confessions,* which date to the fourth century, are written in the form of a prolonged act of repentance. In it, the author discloses his sins, and his sorrow about his sins, to God, asking to be forgiven and made whole again. Confessional magazines of the early twentieth century were likewise designed to enforce morality. They featured stories primarily of women who committed some act of life-ruining indiscretion – adultery, for example – going on to regret their actions, repent and learn the lesson of obedience. Both the magazines *True Story* and *True Confessions* continued publishing as late as 2017, and the genre has been rightly identified and criticised as a means of disciplining women and codifying norms that vilified their sexuality.

Despite its murky origins, the real emancipatory potential of the confessional mode began to be acknowledged in the middle of the twentieth century. Although still a gendered form, confessional writing allowed the author to speak out of traditionally silent spaces: the domestic sphere, and from societal margins. The form allows its authors to make tricky disclosures, such as about abuse (I think of a book I read as a child, Augusten Burroughs' *Running With Scissors*), sexual assault (I think of Roxane Gay's *Hunger*), individuals' histories in the sex work industry (my friend Chloe Higgins' *The Girls*), or abortion (such as that described in Irene Vilar's *Impossible Motherhood*). In 1976, for example, Maya Angelou disclosed publicly for the first time in her memoir *Gather Together in My Name* that she had been a sex worker in her youth: it was important to her and her family, despite her doubts, that she write in an unvarnished manner about her survival and success in a society designed to oppress poor Black women. Later, reflecting on the work, Angelou shared an anecdote of a young Black sex worker who arrived at one of her book signings, and told Angelou that her writing had given her hope; it had made her feel seen.

As online platforms collapse some of the boundaries between public and private means of documenting one's inner state, fears arise that we are increasingly losing the moral or political edge that made the literary confession not the end, but the means to a greater critique: whether a puritanical one aimed at enshrining conservative sexual mores, or a more radical one aimed at subverting patriarchy and racial capitalism. The practices of blogging and micro-blogging, popularised by websites such as LiveJournal, Medium and Tumblr, were, in their foetal state, conceived to enable the curation of an intimate space maintained for only a handful, a means of updating family and friends only. As these platforms have expanded, the audience of such documents has widened to include the public, while the style of the content, fundamentally personal, has altered little.

In 2015, Laura Bennett, writing for *Slate*, coined the term 'first-person industrial complex' to refer to the economy that had blossomed around the genre of online writing that prized confession. At the time, websites such as *xoJane* and *Jezebel* accepted submissions in the 'true story' or 'it happened to me' genre, and its ethics became hotly debated. Although part of a long historical trend inaugurated by magazines such as *True Story* and *True Confessions*, editors involved in the publication of these tales, such as Jia Tolentino, began to voice concerns arising out of the fact that these pieces were increasingly un-curated and un-edited. The writing also did not enjoy the lead times that work published through traditional publishing did, no longer affording the author a 'cooling off' period for serious contemplation of the social consequences that the publication of a piece – containing revelations of racism, incest or criminal activities – might induce.

As readers and writers – such as Tolentino, who began as an editor at *Jezebel* before moving to the *New Yorker* and publishing her essay collection *Trick Mirror* in 2019 – transition between the online and traditional publishing spheres, they can no longer be said to be separate. And so they risk being absorbed into the same circuits of capital which demand virality, and are geared towards milking us for all the content we contain. To not shut the fuck up when someone wants you to is powerful. However, to speak, when asked to speak by market forces, in circumscribed ways, feels more like telling on yourself. Confessional writing is prized, yes, but it is also demanded, and this demand for ever-more unfiltered work creeps into all spheres of publishing, to the point that the honesty of the work increasingly supersedes other artistic concerns.

In 2017, journalist and memoirist Alex Tizon published what was to be his final work. It appeared as the cover story for the June issue of *The Atlantic*, and was entitled 'My Family's Slave'. The work narrated the author's experience being raised by a woman named Eudocia Tomas Pulido, but whom the author knew as Lola. Tizon tells of growing up and slowly piecing together that Lola was the family's personal slave, and realising that she was prevented, by her domestic duties and lack of personal documents, from travelling back to her home, a status quo which was maintained by the family for over five decades. The confession was made possible by Tizon's death. The piece went viral. Initially, I watched it be lauded as an aesthetic feat: beautiful because of its 'honesty'. Following this wave of praise was an avalanche of critique, which noted that fessing up to being a slave-owner was not meritorious in and of itself.

In 2018, writer Junot Diaz published an essay in the *New Yorker* entitled 'The Silence: The Legacy of Childhood

Trauma'. In it, Diaz disclosed publicly for the first time that he had been raped when he was eight years old. He situated this confession inside a second confession of 'hurting other people in the process' of grappling with this serious trauma. In similar fashion to Tizon, the piece went viral, and was at first embraced as important, raw and vulnerable: I know this is how I felt upon reading it, like it was vital that we observe a moment of silence for the gravity of the disclosure. But then, following escalating accusations of sexual misconduct and misogyny levelled at Diaz from female writers, his contemporaries, primarily Black women and women of colour, the piece was re-appraised as theatre: arse-covering, an attempt to hide behind authenticity in order to pre-empt critique.

In these two instances, some readers have judged that the naming of an act cannot trigger absolution in and of itself. Rather, it risks narrating a wrong without analysing the wrong, or stepping into more material practices of accountability that entail true justice. Without devolving into a discussion about the line between repentance and penance – as my goal is not to moralise – my concern in raising these examples is to call attention to the way that artistic judgements are increasingly made on the basis of the quantity of confessions contained within a work.

The Norwegian writer Karl Ove Knausgard has sold books in the order of millions. His work is described as uncomfortably honest, deeply exposing, unflinching and unsparing and shockingly frank. Reviewers remark that he describes moments of 'near-rape' and 'attraction to inappropriately young women', and that he has hurt many of the people around him. But, they note, because he is an open book, because his style is sloppy by design, because there is not a fault that he won't cop to having, criticism cannot touch the work. An aesthetic determination is made on the basis of how much is said, and not what is said, or how. When they do not lift the lid on a zone of silence, but rather only amplify a cultural chorus, admitting to something shocking – such as mistreating a woman – becomes, in my view, not that shocking.

To be clear, I am not calling for a revival of the morality tale, or demanding that we as a society need to rediscover shame. Rather, I hope to note the danger of hiding behind verisimilitude, when it leads to doing nothing with one's admission but waving it about. To do this is to yield to the demand made by capital that we disclose mindlessly. As these disclosures become increasingly de-linked from how they refer to real-world relations of power, they encourage a descent into discourse.

The Pleasure of the Confession

I don't mean to sound like a techno-pessimist. I get it: Foucault is not my dad and so I need not let him tell me what to do. I admit that it is possible that critical theorists may be out of touch on this one. Some of these folks are the types who are startled every time they mistakenly activate voice command, and their phone gurgles 'Sorry, I didn't quite get that'; whereas the rest of us are just thrilled to have someone to talk to.

The problem is I can't make up my mind about confession. I am writing Schrodinger's memoir. I write in fits and bursts, and then I delete it. Maybe I'm fearful-avoidant; maybe I want you to come closer but to also go away. It is possible that I take pleasure in disclosure until it yields discomfort, and then there's a million reasons why it's problematic. The fact is that confession is the (historically contingent) yearning of my soul and to suggest otherwise would be self-denial.

During this crisis, I have spent tens of hours with my dear friends on Zoom completing questionnaires and personality quizzes, collaborating on our answers and picking apart the results: What fictional character are we? What *Seinfeld* character are we? What sense are we (touch)? How do our astrological charts impact our compatibility with one another? What are our attachment styles? What is our Myers–Briggs type (ISTJ)? What is our Harry Potter Myers–Briggs type? What Dungeons and Dragons alignment are we (chaotic good)? What are our schemas? My friend puts together a spreadsheet standardising our results – we make fun of him for being unable to spell the word *subjugation,* and he makes fun of me for scoring so highly in it – so that we can understand our scores better:

	Eda	Difference from avg		Difference from avg		Difference from avg
Emotional Dep	11	−1.1	4	−3.4	13	3.4
Entitlement	11	−1.1	11	3.6	9	−0.6
Abandonment	6	−6.1	8	0.6	6	−3.6

	Eda	Difference from avg		Difference from avg		Difference from avg
Defectiveness	11	−1.1	6	−1.4	4	−5.6
Subjucation	12	−0.1	7	−0.4	7	−2.6
Unrelenting Std	15	2.9	11	3.6	16	6.4
Mistrust Abuse	15	2.9	4	−3.4	12	2.4
Self Sacrifice	16	3.9	8	0.6	10	0.4
Average	12.1		7.4		9.6	

I have successfully gotten each one to hassle their mother to request their birth time, in order to sign them up for a Co-Star profile. On one occasion, a friend had to fossick through his house and dig up his birth documents to find this information. He flicked through the blue baby book for us, holding it faced up to the camera, to walk us through each page. It reminded me of show-and-tell and being a child. These activities build intimacy in safe ways, with oneself and others. It's easier to say 'I'm Severus Snape, LOL: dutiful and loyal and with greasy hair' than to say that 'I was raised via my mother's belief that she would be left to die alone, and much of my upbringing involved daily reminders that I must never abandon her'.

When I religiously read my Co-Star horoscope, it is not because I view the app's insights as determinative. Rather, it is because I think of these technologies as heuristics for learning not only more about oneself, but also learning to understand and to be a good friend to those who 'believe in that sort of thing'. Undeniably, the insights of this application inform many young people's behaviours and self-perception, and if we accept that identity is performative or constitutive – in other words, that it is brought into being by discourse – then this is important. For me, I find it meditative to click through 105 questions that ask me to evaluate myself from many angles. This gentle probing constitutes a form of self-inquiry, and it facilitates one to learn not just that they are caught somewhere halfway between Elaine Benes and George Costanza, but also to liberate hidden truths about oneself. I can't think of anyone who doesn't thrill in being told about themselves, and these data-mining confessional exercises are just new ways of being seen.

Where medieval Catholics used to have to recount to a priest every one of their sexual thoughts, words, acts and positions, we now tell the void. My purity score is 54.1. I didn't know that until now. It's likely that you don't care, although you may now complete this test yourself. Somehow I think the priests may not have been so apathetic about this information. Perhaps it might have gotten back around the town and I would have been locked in a pillory for a day. The void doesn't care if you're a slut.

I like those online confessional practices that erode the 'I' of the self. Anonymous posting, for example on confession pages, is rife, and allows us to speak without inducing the usual social consequences. I don't know anyone from my peer group in secondary school who didn't peruse PostSecret, nor a single peer from university who didn't read our institution's confession page, ironically or not searching for their name among the disclosures of missed connections and crushes, or for validation about collectively despised teachers. And I think these forms of speech might get us closer to breaking out of our subject positions, and help us to speak in less circumscribed ways.

When I look at the online advice subreddits r/relationships and r/AmItheAsshole, the most popular posts are those that involve an individual who is grappling with a romantic partner who so clearly must be broken up with that it inspires spectacle. On one particularly memorable post about the seemingly mundane, but actually quite abusive, exchange of Christmas gifts between husband and wife, the wife in question finally commented, after 1,600 responses: 'I think I need to admit how unhappy with my marriage I am. I'm sorry if my replies are increasingly short. Thanks again everyone. It's a pretty hard wake-up call that people see these glaring problems I've been avoiding. This advice is all appreciated and welcome.' Part of me doubts that these individuals would ever name their uneasiness, the things that they suspect but won't admit, in the absence of the relative anonymity afforded by the internet. The poster emerges out the other end a changed self, not just modified, in Foucault's words, by the act of confession, but more importantly re-constituted by the validation of thousands of others: a public way of being known, yes, but also a means of yielding into the public sphere what some have wished remained private.

That brings me back to the beginning. When I say that people like for you (not) to talk about trauma and that I'm going to talk about it forever and ever and ever, and also never again, what I mean is this: within a singularly confessing society, being a confessing individual is not so singular. It is the price of entry: I pay it in order to exist.

Doğduğun Yer, Doyduğun Yer

Cherry: I know all your gorgeous family in Karachi.

Omar: You've been there?

Cherry: You stupid. What a stupid. It's my home. How could anyone in their right mind call this silly little island off Europe their home? ... Oh God, I'm sick of hearing about these in-betweens. People should make up their minds where they are.

– Hanif Kureishi, *My Beautiful Laundrette*

I have coffee with a student after the semester ends. We get along, somehow, although he is five years my junior at least, and has the habit of walking into the classroom and turning the air conditioner off as his first order of business every week, ignoring that it is me who has turned it on, moments before, and he connects every discussion that we have back to Pablo Escobar, whose business acumen he admires. My student insists on paying for our coffees and we nearly come to blows over it, but he wins out. He points to his Rolex, something I once remarked was *nice* in class, after which he told me how much it cost and I mimed being shot in the chest.

'Fine,' I say. 'But in general you should let your teachers buy these things for you.'

We sit in the sun by the oval and I stare at a magpie that I have watched grow up over the past few weeks as it struts by: his feathering is that of a teenager. I think about how I love this university because it is full of these in-between adolescent creatures.

My student asks me where I grew up and I say Blacktown.

'How funny,' he says. 'My family owns a strip mall out there.' I gawp. We fall into a pattern I find easy: 'You said you were of Turkish background, right?' 'Yes.' 'I love it there.' 'Oh, wow!' – as if I am grateful people know my homeland's name – 'When did you last visit?' '2017. You?' '2012.'

I omit that I fear I am likely to be arrested or detained, if I tried to go again; I stage this discussion with my PhD supervisor often, how arrogant it is or isn't of me to be wary that my research is controversial enough to be noticed. It's not his fault. So I leave him to keep enjoying the things I cannot: skiing holidays, gözleme, hot air balloons that float over Cappadocia in the summer.

*

On exile, Edward Said writes, 'We come to nationalism and its essential association with exile. Nationalism is an assertion of belonging in and to a place, a people, a heritage. It affirms the home created by a community of language, culture and customs; and, by so doing, it fends off exile, fights to prevent its ravages.'

My memories of that final visit in 2012, which I took, fresh out of high school, to visit a loved one, are not happy ones, but they are potent ones. My brain cannot seem to parse the distinction, and their headiness prompts yearning to go back. I don't know where the yearning comes from, but it is one of my few deeply felt emotions. When I have taken MDMA, I have watched as my friends turn to one another, rhapsodise about how much they love each other, their partners, sing them songs, kiss them softly on the mouth or wander off to a bedroom to have slow and spacey sex. By contrast, my thoughts go first to my family, and my sense of our bond throbs between the two poles of respect and understanding, and pain and shared loss. And then my thoughts circle around to İzmir. In 2017, I wrote this, while high: 'I feel a weighty intensity and strength of affiliation with Turkey that actually means nothing because it exists in my imaginary so I have to put it down from my imaginary onto another imaginary and hope that you can share the same feeling, like asking you to taste food the way that I taste food.' I recognise that this is humiliating, and incoherent to boot – far and away more embarrassing than if I were to simply have chemsex, or, in other words, to be where I am, and to be there with who I'm with. In one formulation, you get to come; in the other, you never arrive.

I yearn and I long but it does not relate to any identifiable nationalist instinct. I remember standing in Dolmabahçe

Palace with a loved one, in 2012. She was taking me around
all the common tourist spots, traipsing the same spots she had
shown already to an American friend when he had visited
only a month prior. We stepped into a room that houses
Atatürk's death chambers, the bed made up with a red sheet
bearing the Turkish flag, and it took me a long time to notice
that my companion had gone so still and silent because
tears were rolling down her cheeks. When my mother and
I watch a YouTube show together, from a Turkish comedian
who does a ventriloquist act, she quickly asks me to turn it
off because I'm not laughing. He is sending up mandatory
milli güvenlik classes, delivered weekly to high schoolers
until they were discontinued in 2012. The classes were run
by colonels and retired officers who lectured on military life
and national security. My mother laughs remembering the
way all the kids had to shoot up as soon as the subay entered
the room, stand ramrod straight, and that they would be hit
if they did not wear their hats, which imitated those worn
by the officers: firm brimmed like a peak cap. She collapses
into peals when she remembers how she hated wearing hers,
would hide the hat under her arm, and then she turns to me
and says, 'Siz bu eğitimi görmediniz. Belki o yüzden bizim
gibi milliyetçi olamadınız. You weren't educated the way we
were. Maybe that's why you didn't come out a nationalist the
way we did. Köklerimiz farklı. Our roots are different.'

I do attend school in İzmir in 2000, but only for all of
three days, my mother enrolling my sister and me because
we have been out of school for nearly two months and she
is worried we will fall behind. We get the morning shift,

the school's enrolment so large that it runs two school sessions a day, and our classes begin at 7.30 am. I almost get used to the rush to buy ayran and a sucuk sandwich from the canteen before we mill in the quadrangle to sing the national anthem, me mouthing the first lines before I fall silent because I don't know the rest of the words. My sister eases in in a way I cannot, quickly becoming popular among her peers, while I struggle instantly to keep up with the schoolwork – we seem endlessly to be taking notes off the blackboard, which are written up by the teacher and then erased so quickly that by the time I am done ruling a line in the margin of my page in red pencil, we have already moved on to the next thing. I sit in the back of the class with the boys, one of whom keeps propping his arms up on two desks and swinging over to try to kiss me. I turn my cheek and he headbutts me in my glasses, an early experience that I am sure diverted me from heterosexuality. The girls, for their part, think I am an oddity, asking me for my name, my father's name, my mother's name, and then they call me by my mother's name for reasons I don't understand, giggling and running away after eating handfuls of my lunch that I offer up freely on the playground. I try to avoid using the toilets and hold everything in for seven hours for two days straight. On the third day I am busting, so I decide to bite the bullet and try to adjust to the squat toilets, but all I do is end up pissing on my feet and it soaks into my shoes. The boy who kisses me is reprimanded, hit with a ruler. My mother explains that when she was younger, teachers would require students to hold out their hand, palm facing upwards with their fingers curved out, so that they could be rapped smartly on the tips of their nails, to make it hurt even more. I don't like being bad at school – here, I don't even get to be smart, which makes going home hungry and smelling of piss much worse – so I quit.

When neighbourhood kids stop by the apartment, calling up to our balcony from the streetfront to come out and play, they only ask for my sister. I get used to accompanying her anyway, and we play endless games of saklambaç, substituting 'Ready or not, here I come!' for 'Önüm arkam sağım solum sobe!' I know that this is how my eldest sister grew up, playing marbles in the streets of Tire, returning home every day covered in dust and mud. Once, she explains that she had caused a small riot to break out at her school, having won all the marbles from her male schoolmates, who formed a vendetta against her and began issuing threats. In response, she had spoken to all the neighbours' boys, who showed up one afternoon at her school, despite the fact they attended a different one in a different town, to protect her. I love these stories, love being a part of these stories, which connect me to a place that I'm from that I'm not really from.

I turn off the ventriloquist and put on a Tolga Karaçelik film instead, but my mother asks me to shut that off too, thinks I'm doing it to humour her. When I insist I know and love the director's films, I swear I do, she tells me to just put on something English. I watch *Gişe Memuru* alone.

*

When our cab driver finds out we are from Australia, he explains that although he has been all around the world he hasn't made it as far as Sydney yet. Through the rest of Europe, yes, and even through south-east Asia. He pauses to confirm his suspicion that Justin is south-east Asian, and Justin complies, in that overly blokey manner that I never saw him do unless he was trapped in tight confines with another bloke, or whatever term is its German cognate.

I feel shitty about that question – *Where are you from?* – although I recognise it is valid in the context that, in Berlin, we are indeed foreigners. But I still ask, 'Where are *you* from?'

He tells us Bremen, looking at me as I look at him in the rear-view mirror. I know my face looks sallow, almost scaly, maybe lizard-adjacent. Thirty-five hours of commuting has dried me out like a prune, the moisture having long exited my skin as a result of the unending blasts of re-circulated airplane air and the tiny cups of airplane water that are the opposite of bottomless: all bottom. In a few minutes I will fall into a dead sleep, as soon as my head hits the pillow of our Airbnb in Kreuzkölln, and Justin will go out to get us kebabs, stirring me only for long enough that I can mainline it while prostrate, like being intubated. The cabbie, still watching me, asks, 'Are you pure Australian?' and I say, 'I'm Turkish.'

In a perverse way I'm excited. For weeks prior to our departure I had been coming up behind Justin, tapping him on the shoulder as he diligently worked on some task, and miming that he take out his earphones.

'Yes?' he would ask.

'Are you not keen?' I would ask.

'For what?'

'For me to cop racism as badly as you do.'

His answers cycled through three options: 'Why would I be?', 'Do you think people will be able to tell you're Turkish?' and 'You've already asked me that.'

The cab driver's mood shifts, or maybe my mood shifts, and he says, 'Oh.' And then he starts to explain, almost apologetically, 'I don't know about how it is in Australia, but in Germany, the Turks, they live in ghettoes. They keep themselves away from the rest of the population. They cause lots of problems. It's because they really did not ever adapt to life here. They can go to Turkey every summer, you know, a big exodus. They take their cars and they just drive back home.'

It is my turn to say 'oh'. Justin takes over, impressing the driver with his knowledge of trivia about things blokes are interested in: fishing, The Beatles. We get out of the cab in front of the Airbnb, and I spot a street pole with a bin attached, which I photograph and send to my mother, my final act for the evening: it is one of those bright yellow Berlin bins, and I can't tell if it's designed specifically for dog shit or not. Europeans love dogs, I notice. It seems abusive to force them to live in these cramped apartments. They're creatures who can't live without you, but they are impossible to make happy when they are with you, because you don't even have control over the way you live – intractable. Dog ownership is intractable, I think, realising that I feel a scribble of bleakness, or encroaching madness, even when thinking about dogs, when I am tired like this. I send it to her because there is writing adhered to the front of the bin, which reads Çöpü içine at, Mehmet. I had noticed another further up the block, which read the same thing in English: Put it in the bin, Sam.

'Ne güzel,' I write. 'Toplumsal katılımı sağlıyorlar.' I am being half-sarcastic.

My mother writes back right away. 'Pislikler! Soyledim sana. Oradaki Türkler köyden geliyor. Hatırlatmadan çöplerini bile atamiyorlar.'

I consider arguing with my mother's interpretation of the bins but don't. Who's to say which it is? I have no real insight. My brain supplies *No real binsight*, and I laugh to myself as I drift off.

*

I look up Bremen later and learn that the largest ethnic minority in the region are Turks, making up nearly 7 per cent of the population. Post-war and until the eighties, a large proportion of these migrant labourers worked in the ship-building industry, keeping afloat Bremen's maritime trade. After the closing of the shipyard, they or their children were plunged into some of the highest rates of poverty and unemployment in the country, developing a reputation for relying on social assistance and exploiting the generosity of the German welfare state. This is one of the key stereotypes that proliferates about Germany's kanaks, a slur for Middle Easterners in the country, first applied to Turkish guest workers. Beginning with this programme, Germany has carefully cultivated a reputation for itself, augmented under Merkel in the wake of the Syrian civil war, as a country uniquely accepting of migrants, or at least migration. But the country has not made peace with, nor provided any real inroads to inclusion to, a population whose tenure in the country is almost half as long as the nation-state's entire lifespan. Access to citizenship has been tightly regulated for decades, at first requiring blood descent from a German parent, and later a confirmation of loyalty to the German state, whereby even German-born Turks were required to give up Turkish citizenship in order to naturalise. This has cemented Turkish-Germans' status as in, but not of, Germany – that is, as Ausländer – and today it is not un-common to hear Turks in the country spoken about as unassimilable, as living in a parallel society, refusing to modernise, civilise or integrate. This racialisation is now twofold, having started with Turks' proletarian positioning in society – as migrant workers, and therefore a permanent socioeconomic underclass – and accelerated, particularly post-9/11, by their religious difference.

I am keenly aware that I have been racialised differently living here in Australia. There is no slur that I have been called that targets my specific race, for example, and even my father has only ever been called *Lebo* or *wog*. In high school, I was regularly counted as one of the 'half-white' students, alongside another Turkish boy; these audits were conducted regularly by my classmates because, being a selective high school in the Hills District of Sydney, we were 98 per cent CALD, and it was important to know who was white in order to assess who should be granted easy access to popularity, romantic interest and leadership positions.

In 2014, when I was living in Spain, I met a German woman who acted indifferent to me until she found out I was Turkish, after which she treated me with open vitriol and disgust. Months after that first encounter, we passed each other in a hallway at the Universidad Autónoma de Madrid, where we were both studying, and I watched her pick a hunk of chicken that had fallen out of a sandwich that she had clutched in her hand up off the floor and eat it. *Who's more disgusting, me or you?* I thought, although I pretended not to have noticed, to allow her to save face, or rather to keep stuffing her face. If not for Dirty Sandwich Girl I may not have invested the hours I have, since, attempting to apprehend what it means to be Turkish – to understand oneself as racially oppressed, or not – in different times, different places.

Turkishness is a perfect exemplar of the way that racial categories shift and morph, being pulled to and fro depending on the needs of whiteness. Turkey was one of the first favourite destinations of the orientalists, scholars who travelled to the Eastern world in the eighteenth and nineteenth centuries to produce knowledge about this far-flung land's customs and norms. As Sabrina Strings notes in her book *Fearing the Black Body: the Racial Origins of Fat Phobia,* Turks were, although deemed other, nevertheless commented upon as 'shineingly white' in the eighteenth century. By the nineteenth century, their corpulence and savagery was emphasised instead, in contrast to the 'streamlined aesthetic of the Germans'. Once considered one of the centres of the orient, Turkey started to be viewed in the late twentieth century instead as a middle-point, a bridge between the east and the west. This reappraisal is the result of geopolitics. During the Cold War, Turkey sat on the fringes of the west's idea of itself. Rather than allow it to fall to communism, the United States and Europe preferred to pull the country into the western sphere in order to consolidate against the Soviet bloc. If you travel east of Turkey, you fall off the edge of civilisation. This travel-guide characterisation still plagues perceptions of the country, whose cosmopolitan west coast is widely regarded as liberal, modern, while the south-east of the country is viewed as its rural, backwards, hick cousin, a perception itself driven by the dynamics of domestic racism against Kurds, who live in higher concentrations inland and to the south-east.

Turkishness itself is a fiction, having not gained modern meaning as a social category until it began to be used by Europeans in the late 1800s, by westerners studying the orient. Prior to this, Turks in the region readily mixed with indigenous groups and were not differentiable from them. This is not to say that none of this means anything, or to repeat the platitude that we are all one race, the human race. Indeed, race is real to those who live it. Rather, I emphasise that race is contingent because it allows us to see that other worlds are always possible, that things could always be otherwise. Furthermore, I think that we can best disturb our fixed ideas about race by unravelling it at the edges. I poke and prod at Turkishness until I am satisfied with the conclusion that racialisation is a function of migration and class and worker histories, as well as time. Although I do not think of myself as white right now, there may be a possible future where that is no longer the case. I scrolled through enough heated online arguments during my first years as an undergraduate in autonomous spaces for people of colour, as we litigated the question of whether Italians or Greeks were white or not, to know that whiteness is a moving target, and that entry to whiteness is granted to populations like the Irish, Italians and occasionally even Turks, as a function of their positioning in the class structure. This explains why, for example, Poles – a large precarious, poor, migrant worker population – are currently increasingly subject to racist attacks in the UK.

Yet another one of the epic arguments Tex and I stage at the office concerns this question, when I insist that nothing about physical appearance has any bearing on race. He remarks that he finally thinks I've lost it, and I insist that Blackness is first and foremost a socially invented category, to justify the exploitation of certain peoples, well before it is a phenotype, and I repeat the well-worn adage that there is more genetic variation *within* racial groupings than *between* them. I feel this especially because my appearance has never changed in my lifetime – beyond that I have developed a deep forehead furrow – but the way that my appearance is racialised, or not, has changed. I point out to him that I recall not thinking of myself as racialised until after 9/11, when all the kids, like myself, who attended Muslim scripture classes, were treated by a few of the boys, suddenly, as if we were disgusting – one not wanting to touch a book that I had touched because I had touched it, a change that overcame him as if overnight. Before this, as far back as 1922, when the Australian Department of Home and Territories made the decision to naturalise Turks and bring their status in line with that of 'other Europeans', we were indeed almost white.

I finally become convinced I have to go to Germany – twist my arm, I'll go to Germany! – after Justin is gifted a copy of *The Strange Death of Europe* by Douglas Murray, a farewell present from an employer he left at the end of 2017. In it, Murray criticises the policies of European countries who have allowed excessive numbers of migrants, particularly Muslim ones, onto their shores, and laments the negative impacts this change in European demography is having on the cultural values and social fabric of European civilisation, namely its putative liberalism and secularism. The author notes that, at its closest point, five miles is all that separates Turkey from Europe. He discusses the failure of the German guest-worker programme that never saw these temporary populations go back home. Instead, he emphasises that in key European cities, in countries like the Netherlands, France and Germany, which are regularly cited as bastions of multiculturalism, there are mini-Turkeys, Muslim enclaves, where the birth and crime rates are high and the women oppressed.

I don't understand why Justin has been gifted *The Strange Death of Europe*, which I read in a rage. Justin says, 'They probably didn't see you,' he points at me, 'in this,' he points at the book.

I wonder if my cabbie has ever set foot in the poor Bremen neighbourhoods of Gröpelingen, Lindenhof, Ohlenhof, which are often dubbed 'Little İstanbul'. It's funny how you can say you are from a city, but really be from a grid of social life that extends three streets wide by three streets long. I wonder who it is that is really holding themselves apart from the other. The thing about the idea of the ethnic enclave is this: in order to secure a centre, they push you to the margins, and then they blame you for cultivating an existence there.

*

The Turkish diasporic neighbourhoods that I am interested in on this trip, namely Neukölln and Kreuzberg, are gentrifying rapidly, as streets once deemed too dangerous to walk down are reimagined as grungy in that fashionable way that attracts alternate youths. This is part of the reason Justin and I stay where we do, right between the two of them. All his friends in Sydney, who have done stints in Berlin – the kind that involves camping out front of Berghain and snorting ketamine off toilet seats – recommend the area for its food, its arts scene, its affordability, its vibe. I snicker, 'Wow, this is the gritty urban realism your friends told us about,' after we walk past a man hidden in a nook on a street corner, proclaiming loudly into his phone, 'Sana hızlandırıcı satabilirim,' assuming that neither of us will understand he is selling drugs to his mate on the other end. On the next street we pass a homeless man who, when I hand him a five-Euro note, murmurs, 'Allah kalbine göre versin.'

It is obvious to me that I am a beneficiary of this gentrification, not one of the area's Turkish originals. It is obvious in the way that when Justin and I step into Imren Grill – widely regarded as a Berlin institution, and which attracts food tourists from surrounding areas – and I order in Turkish, the proprietor still calls me hanımefendi even though I am very obviously at least three decades his junior. In (yet) another kebab shop, that bears the very Ottoman name Şehzade, I fall into conversation with the staff, one of whom, upon learning that my family ended up in Australia, not Germany, remarks, 'Wow, Sidney denen yer gerçekten de var mıymış?' as if I am an alien. I buy Justin a spezi döner, which is Berlin's answer to the halal snack pack, the key difference between the two meals being that the final layer of the spezi döner is hot, wet salad. I am not convinced from the perspective of taste about the recombination of these ingredients, although I appreciate their originality. Justin thinks my brain is cooked for describing a box of meat as sui generis.

In my notes on this trip, I write, 'All the conditions that make Kreuzberg and Neukölln appealing to newcomers and tourists are things that the locals might have different if they could: it feels like a little Turkey due to segregation; it feels gritty because the housing is dense and of lower quality; there are cheap food joints because that's the job that you have to do and the price you have to sell it for.'

At Maybachufer market I almost feel whatever feeling it is I am seeking to feel. It almost recreates the smell of the pazar, which we visited every week in 2000, and then again in 2012. Here I can finally put my finger on what the scent is, and I realise it's just fresh vegetables, mostly capsicum. It's silly that my affective memory is so moved by the smell of bell peppers, a food I would generally turn my nose up at. I buy us sigara böreği and we hold them in our gloved hands, me enjoying the way it warms my fingers through the wool, and we roam the tight crush of stalls slowly. Then I drop my sigara böreği on the floor, and it brings tears to my eyes, and I refuse to go back to get another. That evening, I write that Maybachufer is a 'simulation upon which "unoriginality" bricolages'. In retrospect, I don't know what I meant by this – it is possible I was just hungry.

*

Turkish–Australian scholar Orhan Karagoz writes that

> even the second-generation, educated Turkish people
> believe that it is an obligation to regularly visit Turkey in
> order to preserve one's Turkishness. There are no explicit
> sanctions for those who do not regularly visit Turkey,
> though they may become the subject of gossip and may
> be presented as selfish, materialistic, compromising their
> Turkishness and becoming an 'Aussie' ... The perception
> of Turkey as a place to charge one's Turkishness is linked
> to the concept of the motherland ... Many perceive
> Turkey as a fantasy land compared to life in Australia,
> a place where Turks can feel more alive, spend money

freely, and fulfil dreams ... [T]he homeland is the
existential centre for Turkish-Australians, which enables
them to recharge their Turkishness when they return.

Motherland as a repository of authenticity; motherland
as a fictive home; motherland as a site on which to pin
longing. One of the terms for unattainable longing is
saudade. Much is made of this word in literary circles
because it is deemed untranslatable, and we fetishise the
untranslatable – the notion that there might be something
so foreign to us that we could never hope to grasp it. Inside
this drive – to capture the uncapturable – lies poetry, I
suppose; attempts to distil the affect of *saudade* spawn
verse, books, music. Nostalgia or homesickness is to feel a
longing deeply, to code it as pleasant because it vivifies a
sense of connectedness to a place, or a time, or a person,
thought lost. What *saudade* captures is that you can't
ever recreate it, this lost thing: it is indeed forever gone.
More importantly, I think, the thing about attempting to
capture the uncapturable – whether that be the meaning of
a foreign word, or a lost time, person or place – is that if
we had it we could not continue to want it. Maybe it is the
Lacanian in me, but I have grown to believe that beyond the
yearning and longing lies no further gratification, that they
are their own reward. Consummation of desire is possibly
always disappointing – the place you grew up is not as you
remember it, you are reminded why you hated your friends
enough to leave, your ex still chews with his mouth open,
and so on. It is sad, maybe not in the exact same way, but

close, to how we get bummed after we orgasm, how the climax rarely feels as good as its anticipation.

Of late I have decided that I am chasing gurbet, circling in an attempt to distil its untranslatable essence. In Turkish there is the phrase, gurbet çekmek. Çekmek is a verb that means both to pull or tow or drag, but also to suffer. You might say you çek pain, or that you are suffering from gurbet, that is, distance from one's home. Gurbet çekmek is to suffer from being in diaspora, which means to suffer from longing – hasret – for one's home as well as to suffer the difficulties of being a foreigner. I curate a Spotify playlist entitled Gurbet, because there is a cornucopia of Turkish songs on the subject, referring both to distance from one's love and one's homeland, or memleket. The two most significant of these, to me, are 3 Hürel's 'Yara' and Özdemir Erdoğan's 'Gurbet', both released, I think not coincidentally, in the early 1970s, and both naming, in their lyrics, gurbet as a wound, an originary wound. I listen to these songs and they egg on my Turkey-lust, and I think that I don't know how to long for a home without romanticising that home.

In Turkish there is another saying, which offers a different definition of home, and which makes me sad in its own way. Memleket doğduğun değil, doyduğun yerdir: your homeland is not where you are born, but the place where you grow full. I see it in a documentary Justin and I happen to catch playing at the otherwise unpopulated Currywurst Museum in Berlin: we are goofing around, taking the day off from more serious research I had otherwise been doing for an essay. It's a fond memory I have of the two of us, an experience together that we'll never have again. A Turkish chef who has come to Germany to work, but cannot get a visa – a phenomenon that is hobbling the German food industry – makes this remark: memleket doğduğun değil doyduğun yerdir. In other words, he's saying he's gotta eat. Even though it hurts, we leave our homes, and we find ways to grow sated elsewhere.

*

I meet Cem at a prize ceremony in 2018, where I dutifully read a piece of mine that was published in a Melbourne literary journal. I am receiving a fellowship from the University of Melbourne, and before the event begins, one of the judges, a university lecturer, leans over to me, effusive, kind, supportive, and remarks that I write just like Elif Batuman, which only makes me more delusional about my level of talent.

Cem approaches me afterwards with two women by his side, and greets me easily in Turkish. I feel instant paranoid shame and exposure about my accent, having read a passage in Turkish on stage moments before: I'll never sound native. But I am thrilled, because they are thrilled for me: they insist that we take photos together. One of them is pleased I have mentioned a former friend of mine, from a past life, whom I have strongly implied is gay.

'I'm also gay by implication,' she says. We hug tightly before they depart, and I thank them for being here – not that they were there for me, but rather for a writer, Cem's partner, who had won a more prestigious prize than I had. Cem laughs like it's ridiculous I've managed to avoid them so far, and says, 'If you're looking for Turks, come to Broadmeadows,' and we add each other on Facebook.

In Broadmeadows, in 2021, I stop into the Turkish Islamic and Cultural Centre, wondering at myself. It's a place which, replicated in Sydney – which it is – I would never step into, adorned on the outside with the signage of a Turkish and an Australian flag kissing. A nation as a unit of belonging – and a flag as its visual instantiation – is too large to animate my imaginary. These flags mean much less to me than the 500-metre radius that surrounds my childhood homes in Blacktown. They mean less to me than Auburn's shops, and they mean less to me than every place I have formed a memory with a friend or loved one.

We are separated from each other and from the fantasy of the plenitude of permanent belonging that, I am convinced, exists only in our imaginations, by more than an ocean, but also by class, by politics. I believe that if my parents returned to Turkey, it's likely they would not belong anymore – would not feel that they belong, if they ever felt it. Furthermore, it would depend on the neighbourhood: not just the time, but also the exact place. Communists roam the streets of İstanbul's 1 Mayis neighbourhood. My mother knows little about this brand of leftism because she was raised in a family whose members have, sometimes, supported the fascist MHP party. I laugh when I recall that a Kurdish woman, a Blacktown local, once scoffed when asked to give my mother a lift, remarking, '*That* fascist?' I imagine her driving off into the distance, smoke swirling out of her tailpipe.

I am also angry at these spaces, which are touted as great marshallers of foreigners, and deemed adept at inducing collectivity: the idea that mosques are thrown up in places like Coburg and Auburn to provide refuge to the cities' Muslim communities. But this is also illusory. My father was at one time employed to work on the construction of a mosque in Sydney's western suburbs. When they discovered he was Alevi they let him go; when I see the mosque out the window as I pass it on the Western Line train, my mind stops wandering and I snap to attention and pull back my lips to bare my teeth.

Later, I take in the work of coppersmith Shireen Taweel. We discuss the way that we are both sensitive to place, me as a Turkish-Australian and she as a Lebanese-Australian. She tells me about visiting the oldest standing mosque in Australia, the Afghan Mosque in Broken Hill, built lovingly and devotedly by nineteenth-century camel drivers in Australia, the majority of them Muslim. She emphasises how these Ghans – short for 'Afghans', who made up a portion of the cameleers – extracted materials out of the land, transforming them in order to build themselves these glistening reminders of home. She codes this act as politically distinct from the approach taken by British colonists, viewing it as an attempt to relate to the environment – and to the Indigenous communities the worshipers encountered – rather than seeking to dominate it and use its natural resources to build guns, bombs, or prisons. The conversation brings me, as almost all conversations do, back to trauma. Migration is a trauma, among others, and trauma pulls you away from the world: generates an implacable sense of distance between oneself and everyone else, an estrangement that tells you that you could not possibly be like others, relate to others, or be present where you are. I am trying to fiddle with a new definition of home, with the idea that it is not the same as a homeland.

*

When I first visited Germany in 2014, the guide on the walking tour I was on stood us in front of a cafe at Kottbusser Tor. He seemed to know the Turkish owners, who quickly seated our group and brought us bottles of ayran and gazoz, while he explained that this exact site, pointing to a small square, is where a group of neo-Nazis come to bash people of colour every year, an annual expedition. In the eighties, the 36 Boys gang was formed to defend against such attacks. The gang does not operate anymore, and I learn that, instead, committed antifascists organise counter-rallies on these dates, show up early, scout and fight back when the neo-Nazis show up to Kotti.

On our last day before we leave, Justin and I order a MyTaxi to the airport at 5.45 am. The driver steps out of the same apartment building as us, his first trip of the morning, and we laugh and try to communicate in English about what number flat is his and what number flat was ours, but we cannot quite figure it out. Eventually he just says, 'Komşu,' a word I finally understand, and I respond, 'Türk müsünüz?' but he says no, that he is Azeri. 'Yeterince yakın,' I say, and we are able to conduct something resembling a mutually intelligible dialogue.

When we come back, rounding out our Europe trip with

a few days in Berlin again, I decide that there is an exuberant degeneracy to these suburbs, in the way that they have forced together a such broad cross-section of marginalised groups, and thrown into relief the reality of the composition of the working class: Black people with punks with queers with Turks with Kurds with refugees. Despite accusations that these areas house a conservative impulse – the backwards diaspora preserved in amber – I can see, on the contrary, clear signs of situated, immanent antifascist struggle: we pass several walls graffitied with *Apo*, *YPG*, and *PKK*, references to the imprisoned leader of the Kurdistan Worker's Party (PKK), Abdullah Öcalan, a Kurdish liberation group operating in Turkey that I have been studying since 2016. We are there in 2018, before the Turkish presidential election, and there are stickers adhered to almost every surface on one street in support of the Hayır campaign against Erdoğan. We walk by countless storefronts that have LGBTQIA+ pride flags up alongside posters in Turkish warning Nazis to keep out. Each sticker that gets appliqued and scratched off and reapplied and scratched off and reapplied, and each piece of graffiti that is painted over and thrown up again is a way of marking out this place as a home. I think that this – committed antifascist and anticolonial politics – is one way of being where you are, of not having one foot straddling one continent that does not exist and another another.

*

Auburn, a suburb of Sydney's west within twenty kilometres of Blacktown, is my little Turkey, my particular enclave. The kuyumcu we visit on Station Road when I am a child recalls the kuyumcu we visit in İzmir to stock up on gold before we leave, my mother never satisfied with the quality of the gold here. One of my favourite places to go is the Turkish supermarket on Queen Street, to which my father ducks out when I visit, in order to buy me mantı and sucuk and biber salçası to take home with me back to the Inner West, and where he used to go when I was a child, bringing us back packets of Topkek and Çokoprens, and tubes of Çokokrem, a hazelnut spread that houseguests, when they saw us suckling one down, would regularly mistake for toothpaste. My sister and I, seven and eleven respectively, living in Turkey for several months for the first time ever, taking our first Turkish Airlines flight from İstanbul to İzmir, are relieved when we recognise the complimentary Topkeks we are handed by a flight attendant. When we are living in my grandmother's flat in Üçkuyular in 2000, we get used to being handed change and small notes by some harried adult, and running down together to the bakkal a few blocks away, returning with fresh white bread and Çokokrem. This same Turkish supermarket in Auburn is found, in 2018, to have accepted a delivery of sausage-making machines stuffed with half a tonne of ecstasy; it makes the rounds on social media among the Sydney diaspora, and we all find it hysterical, either the idea that all Turks are indeed drug-dealers, or the image of a large sausage-shaped tube of MDMA hitting the market, a Turkish special. On Station Road, lines curve around the corner at Gaziantep Sweets twice a year on holidays. For Şeker Bayramı and Ramazan my father makes it a ritual to bring home trays weighing several kilograms of baklava, burma, kurabiye, small chocolates filled with nuts that I hide strategically through my bedroom, sometimes in drawers, so I can find them later and drip-feed them to myself for the next several weeks. For the duration of my youth, before my father has a digital set-top box for Turkish TV hooked up at the house by a friend of a friend, we visit a shop called Altın Köprü on Civic Road. Next to it is a store that sells garish Kemalist paraphernalia, which my father scoffs at. We are full of ızgara et or adana, wolfed down at Sofra or, more cheap and cheerful, New Star Kebab, and we are just about to head home, and my father is holding a short list hand-written by my mother on an unevenly torn paper scrap. Inside, the counter is manned by a Turkish fellow who sits in front of a wide shelf lined with videos, meant for a VCR, labelled in white masking tape, written on in black Sharpie things like Çocuklar Duymasın 145. Bolum, Yarım Elma 1. Bolum, Sihirli Annem 12. Bolum. My father dutifully reads out what is on his slip, and the fellow skims his fingers across the tapes, pulling them out with impressive speed, caught halfway between a card dealer and a librarian. I think back fondly to this ersatz Blockbuster, fantasising with admiration about the army of TVs and VCRs it would take to produce these recordings in such volume, to satisfy the viewing habits of the Turkish community, and help them keep up with the dizis as they were airing in the homeland; often, most recent episodes of particularly popular series would be unavailable, all the copies already loaned out, so my family might ask for something more esoteric, a less current dizi, sending the man into the back room to go searching. Then, he'd make a note in a ledger, and we would pay a few dollars per video to take them home, returning them the next week, no doubt to be wiped and recorded over again. My assumption is that this service has died out with the popularisation of online streaming, which even my parents have mastered. But, when I think about Auburn, I wonder most of all what has happened to these tapes, this living archive of the viewing habits of the diaspora in the first decade of the twenty-first century. This Auburn of twenty years ago, as it exists in my mind, does not really remind me of Turkey, now that I have the life experiences to compare. It's not even that it is or is not a poor facsimile, a photocopy of a photocopy. The Auburn of my mind is not a copy, not an attempt to restage or recreate something else, but rather an original: a thing that is itself.

Works Cited

Abdel-Fattah, Randa. 2017. *Islamophobia and Everyday Multiculturalism in Australia*. London: Routledge.

Ahmed, Sara. 2021. *Complaint!* Durham: Duke University Press.

AlphaBeta. 2019. 'Flexibility and Fairness: What matters to workers in the new economy.' March. <alphabeta.com/wp-content/uploads/2019/03/flexibilityandfairness-whatmatterstoworkersintheneweconomy.pdf> Date accessed 9 December 2021.

Amin, Mridula. 2021. 'How "Heat Refuges" Could Help People like Ian Escape Sweltering Days in Western Sydney.' ABC News, 13 January. <www.abc.net.au/news/2021-01-14/western-sydney-heat-refuge-strategy-needed-for-summer-heatwaves/13026882> Date accessed 9 December 2021.

Angelou, Maya. 2004. 'Maya Angelou.' *In A Wealth of Wisdom: Legendary African American Elders Speak*, edited by Camille O. Cosby and Renee Poussaint, 1–6. New York: Simon and Schuster.

Askowitz, Andrea. 2020. 'My Family Are the Lockdown-Breaking Entitled Americans You've Heard About.' 15 May. <www.independent.co.uk/voices/coronavirus-lockdown-breaking-madrid-miami-entitled-americans-a9517476.html> Date accessed 9 December 2021.

Begley, Patrick. 2021. 'The Death Uber Eats Disowned.' *ABC News*, 24 June. <www.abc.net.au/radionational/programs/backgroundbriefing/death-uber-eats-disowned-food-delivery-safety-cyclist/13417942> Date accessed 9 December 2021.

Bennett, Laura. 2015. 'The First-Person Industrial Complex.' *Slate*, 14 September. <www.slate.com/articles/life/technology/2015/09/the_first_person_industrial_complex_how_the_harrowing_personal_essay_took.html> Date accessed 9 December 2021.

Bounds, Michael and Alan Morris. 2005. 'High-rise Gentrification: The Redevelopment of Pyrmont Ultimo.' *Urban Design International*, vol. 10: pp. 179–188.

Works Cited

Burton, Rosamund. 2018. 'The Double Act Working to Save a Heritage Precinct.' *Sydney Morning Herald*, 20 October. <www.smh.com.au/national/nsw/the-double-act-working-to-save-a-heritage-precinct-20181016-p509zi.html> Date accessed 9 December 2021.

Butler, Judith. 1993. *Bodies That Matter: On the Discursive Limits of 'Sex.'* London: Routledge.

Chomsky, Noam. 2013. *Power Systems: Conversations with David Barsamian on Global Democratic Uprisings and the New Challenges to U.S. Empire.* London: Penguin.

Coates, Ta-Nehisi. 2015. *Between the World and Me.* Melbourne: Text Publishing.

Dean, Jodi. 2016. *Crowds and Party.* London: Verso Books.

Debord, Guy. 1967. *The Society of the Spectacle.* Trans. Ken Knabb. Berkeley: Bureau of Public Secrets.

Dillinger, Johannes. 2011. *Magical Treasure Hunting in Europe and North America: A History.* Basingstoke: Palgrave Macmillan.

Edelman, Lee. 2004. *No Future: Queer Theory and the Death Drive.* Durham: Duke University Press.

Fisher, Mark. 2009. *Capitalist Realism: Is There No Alternative?* Hampshire: Zero Books.

Fisher, Mark. 2018. *K-Punk: The Collected Writings of Mark Fisher: The Collected and Unpublished Writings of Mark Fisher.* Edited by Darren Ambrose. London: Repeater.

Foucault, Michel. 1978. *History of Sexuality, Volume 1: An Introduction.* Translated by Robert Hurley. London: Penguin.

Foucault, Michel. 2003. *'Society Must Be Defended': Lectures at the College de France, 1975–76.* Edited by Mauro Bertani and Alessandro Fontana. Translated by David Macey. New York: Picador.

Garner, Dwight. 2015. 'Review: Karl Ove Knausgaard's "My Struggle: Book Four."' *The New York Times*, 20 April. <www.nytimes.com/2015/04/21/books/review-karl-ove-knausgaards-my-struggle-book-four.html> Date accessed 9 December 2021.

Glancy, Josh. 2015. 'Karl Ove Knausgaard: A Traitor to His Family.' 6 November. <www.theaustralian.com.au/world/the-times/karl-ove-knausgaard-a-traitor-to-his-family/news-story/8588890843c7d69a30101aadc4e4d4a1> Date accessed 9 December 2021.

Harris, Josh. 2018. 'Parramatta Residents Fight to Save Heritage Buildings in the Shadow of Powerhouse Museum Move.' *ArchitectureAU*, 5 July. <architectureau.com/articles/parramatta-residents-fight-to-save-heritage-buildings-in-the-shadow-of-powerhouse-museum-move/> Date accessed 9 December 2021.

Hurley, Kelly. 1996. *The Gothic Body: Sexuality, Materialism, and Degeneration at the Fin de Siècle*. Cambridge Studies in Nineteenth-Century Literature and Culture. Cambridge: Cambridge University Press.

Karagoz, Orhan. "Preserving Turkishness in the Daily Life of Broadmeadows." University of Melbourne, 2020, <http://hdl.handle.net/11343/248430>.

Kolk, Bessel van der. 2014. *The Body Keeps the Score: Brain, Mind, and Body in the Healing of Trauma*. New York: Penguin Publishing Group.

Kristeva, Julia. 1982. *Powers of Horror: An Essay on Abjection*. Translated by Leon Roudiez. New York: Columbia University Press.

Lacan, Jacques. 2001. 'The Function and Field of Speech and Language in Psychoanalysis.' In *Écrits: A Selection*, translated by Alan Sheridan, 23–86. London: Routledge.

Lentin, Alana. 2020. *Why Race Still Matters*. Cambridge: Polity Press.

Lewis, Sophie. 2019. *Full Surrogacy Now: Feminism Against Family*. London: Verso Books.

McCarthy, Rebecca. 2017. 'Ninety-Eight Years of Fallen Women.' *The Awl*. 16 August. <www.theawl.com/2017/08/ninety-eight-years-of-fallen-women> Date accessed 9 December 2021.

Murray, Douglas. 2017. *The Strange Death of Europe: Immigration, Identity, Islam*. London: Bloomsbury.

Neuwirth, Robert. 2006. *Shadow Cities: A Billion Squatters, A New Urban World*. London: Routledge.

Newman, Saul. 2018. *Political Theology: A Critical Introduction*. Cambridge: Polity.

Nierenberg, Amelia, and Quoctrung Bui. 2019. 'Chinese Restaurants Are Closing. That's a Good Thing, the Owners Say.' *The New York Times*, 24 December. <www.nytimes.com/2019/12/24/upshot/chinese-restaurants-closing-upward-mobility-second-generation.html> Date accessed 9 December 2021.

O'Sullivan, Matt. 2017. 'Eat Street Restaurants Fear They Won't Survive Parramatta Light Rail Build.' *Sydney Morning Herald*, 19 November. <www.smh.com.au/national/nsw/eat-street-restaurants-fear-they-wont-survive-parramatta-light-rail-build-20170621-gwv8o1.html> Date accessed 9 December 2021.

Pauls, Alan. 2019. 'Mi Lucha, El Libro de La Década (My Struggle, the Book of the Decade).' *La Tercera*, 29 December. <www.latercera.com/la-tercera-domingo/noticia/alan-pauls-lucha-libro-la-decada/955177> Date accessed 9 December 2021.

Plumwood, Val. 2008. 'Shadow Places and the Politics of Dwelling.' *Australian Humanities Review* 44.

Said, Edward W. 2002. *Reflections on Exile and Other Essays*. New Haven: Harvard University Press.

Sedgwick, Eve Kosofsky. 2003. 'Paranoid Reading and Reparative Reading.' In *Touching Feeling: Affect, Pedagogy, Performativity*, edited by Eve Kosofsky Sedgwick and Adam Frank, 123–52. Durham: Duke University Press.

Shure, Marnie. 2020. 'Twitter Implodes over a Charcuterie Board.' *The Takeout*, 8 April. <thetakeout.com/twitter-implodes-over-a-charcuterie-board-1844605669> Date accessed 9 December 2021.

Stevens, Heidi. 2017. '"My Family's Slave" Is Haunting, Essential Reading.' *Chicago Tribune*. 17 May. <www.chicagotribune.com/columns/heidi-stevens/ct-wednesday-balancing-my-familys-slave-20170517-column.html> Date accessed 9 December 2021.

Strings, Sabrina. 2019. *Fearing the Black Body: The Racial Origins of Fat Phobia*. New York: NYU Press.

Swift, Samuel L., M. Maria Glymour, Tali Elfassy, Cora Lewis, Catarina I. Kiefe, Stephen Sidney, Sebastian Calonico, Daniel Feaster, Zinzi Bailey, and Adina Zeki Al Hazzouri. 2019. 'Racial Discrimination in Medical Care Settings and Opioid Pain Reliever Misuse in a U.S. Cohort: 1992 to 2015.' *PLOS ONE* 14, no. 12: 1–12.

Tan, Cher. 2019. 'Demanding Convenience: The False Promise of the On-Demand Economy.' *Kill Your Darlings*, 9 December. <www.killyourdarlings.com.au/article/demanding-convenience-the-false-promise-of-the-on-demand-economy>. Date accessed 9 December 2021.

Taylor, Chloe. 2008. *The Culture of Confession from Augustine to Foucault: A Genealogy of the 'Confessing Animal.'* London: Routledge.

Varoufakis, Yanis. 2018. 'Introduction.' In *The Communist Manifesto: With an Introduction by Yanis Varoufakis*, by Karl Marx and Friedrich Engels. London: Vintage Books.

Wade, Matt, and Danielle Mahe. 2021. '"A Shame on Our City": The Yawning Gap in Lifespans across Sydney.' *The Sydney Morning Herald*, 26 January. <www.smh.com.au/national/nsw/a-shame-on-our-city-the-yawning-gap-in-lifespans-across-sydney-20210124-p56wgp.html> Date accessed 9 December 2021.

Wark, McKenzie. 2019. *Capital Is Dead: Is This Something Worse?* London: Verso Books.

Whittaker, Alison. 2018. Radio interview on Triple R 102.7FM, 19 September.

Western, John. 2016. *Cosmopolitan Europe: A Strasbourg Self-Portrait*. London: Routledge.

Acknowledgments

The years 2020 and 2021, during which I completed the final essays of this book, have been both the hardest and the easiest years of my life. I had a few hard things happen to me when I was younger. I wish I had known the support of the people I have in my life now, then. You have all in your own ways helped drag my carcass through what has turned out to be a very long life, so far, in some cases kicking it over the line. I didn't finish this book, really – you all did.

To my wonderful friends, Jim Clifford, Ellen O'Brien, Hayley Scrivenor, Faith Chaza, Umeya Chaudhuri, Stuart Rollo, Niro Siriwardena, Kai Zen, Cher Tan, Alison Whittaker, Durga Chandran, Rebecca Wong, Sareeta Zaid, Harry Maher, James Kwon, Andrea Lim and newcomers Daniel Gomez and especially Kate Phillips. To the women writers who have, in their own ways, variously mothered or mentored me: Felicity Castagna and Sheila Pham, who brought me into the Western Sydney writing space, unconditionally, and from whom I am always learning; Eileen Chong, my fellow Sagittarian, whose wisdom and heart bolster me greatly; Fiona Wright, who is the kind of essayist I want to be; Ellena Savage and Julie Koh, without whose practical help and profound generosity I could not have navigated this process; Catriona Menzies-Pike, who always makes me seem a lot smarter than I am; and Augusta Supple – you may claim I saved your lockdown, but I think we saved each other. In my other life I am an academic, so I must acknowledge Sarah G Phillips, my PhD supervisor and friend, who has always shown me kindness and regard I am often convinced I do not deserve, and Anna Boucher and Madison Cartwright. And to my parents and family, who I am always trying to understand, not only in order that I can understand myself, but so that I can act with empathy on the world.

I stridently believe everyone should have a publisher like Harriet McInerney, who is a marvel, incredibly patient, and always backed this work even when I was not convinced I could do it.

My thanks to the Australia Council for the Arts, the Harris Endowment for Medical Humanities, Writing NSW, Create NSW and the Neilma Sidney Literary Travel Fund for making this labour possible.

This book was written on Dharug and Gadigal country, land over which sovereignty was never ceded. I have donated $5000 of income made while I developed the essays in this book to Indigenous-led organisations. I acknowledge this not in order to engage in self-congratulation, although I am conscious it may read that way. Rather, I have added this section here, after much consideration, because I believe it is important that, given the themes of this book, namely the repeated emphasis I have tried to place on grounding our politics and our care in the material conditions of people's lives, that I prove that I mean it.

Some of these essays have appeared elsewhere. 'Gothic Body, in Two Parts' in *Voiceworks Online;* 'Only So Much' and 'Live On' in *Meanjin*; 'Rahat' in *The Lifted Brow;* 'Tell-all' and 'Second City' in the *Sydney Review of Books;* 'Shit-Eating' in *Liminal Magazine.* A few paragraphs from 'Kalıtsal' appeared on Footscray Arts Centre's website, under the title 'Born'.

Printed in the USA
CPSIA information can be obtained
at www.ICGtesting.com
BVHW040411140823
668485BV00001B/8